How to
*Un*spoil
Your
Child *Fast*

How to
*Un*spoil
Your
Child *Fast*

A Speedy, Complete Guide to
Contented Children and Happy Parents

Richard Bromfield, PhD

Published by Sourcebooks, Inc.
P.O. Box 4410, Naperville, Illinois 60567-4410
(630) 961-3900
Fax: (630) 961-2168
www.sourcebooks.com

Library of Congress Cataloging-in-Publication Data

Bromfield, Richard.
  How to unspoil your child fast : a speedy, complete guide to contented children and happy parents / by Richard Bromfield.
      p. cm.
  1. Child rearing. 2. Parenting. I. Title.
  HQ769.B6814 2010
  649'.7--dc22

                          2010010672

            Printed and bound in the United States of America.
                  VP 10 9 8 7 6 5 4 3 2 1

To the parents and children who've taught me well.

I swear, my dear, you'll spoil that child.

—Thomas Congreve, 1694

Contents

Acknowledgments

I WISH TO THANK Rochelle Sharpe for reading and advising on an earlier version of the book. Thanks to Whitney Lee for generously carrying my message to parents in other countries. And, most of all, my gratitude goes to Shana Drehs at Sourcebooks whose editorial enthusiasm and wisdom get much of the credit for transforming my original manuscript into this book.

Children today are tyrants. They contradict their parents, gobble their food, and tyrannize their teachers.

—SOCRATES

Introduction

ARE OUR CHILDREN INDULGED AND SPOILED?

Check out the numbers. According to a 2007 survey conducted by AOL and the family magazine *Cookie*, 94 percent of parents say their children are spoiled, up from the 80 percent measured by a 1991 *Time* and CNN poll. This percentage may sound high, but to me the question is, Who are these other 6 percent, and who are they kidding?

Though you might be years from thinking about your child's adolescence, consider these sobering statistics: A Schwab Foundation survey found that 31 percent of teens owe an average of $230, and 14 percent owe more than $1,000! Is it any wonder that about half of these teens expressed concern about whether they would ever be able to repay these debts? In another poll that sampled the wealthiest 1 percent of Americans, 57 percent of parents felt that their children had failed to learn the value of money and how to work for it. And in a Center for a New American Dream survey, a vast majority of parents (87 percent) reported that the consumerism of modern society makes instilling good values in their children a much harder job. That the amount of advertising dollars targeting youths is nearing $20 billion—$20 billion!—and is being aimed at younger children, even toddlers, underscores the fact that parents' fears are well founded.

The numbers don't lie, and there are too many of them to ignore or dismiss as random static or propaganda from any one interest group. The overindulgence that's epidemic in America and most other industrialized countries is an equal-opportunity illness. It plagues the rich, the middle class, and the poor, without regard for a family's race, religion, or politics.

But those are statistics about all children. Let's talk about specific children—children like six-year-old Gabe.

In his short life, Gabe has already made substantial progress in his quest for every set in the Playmobil catalog. Last I heard, Gabe had saved $200 of his "own" money to put toward an expensive Playmobil collector's set that his parents agreed to purchase on his behalf the exact day that he has enough money, a goal he expects to reach quickly.

Callie is a bright kindergartner whose demands and tantrums hold her parents hostage. Callie's intelligent parents struggle through day after day of perpetually surrendering and kowtowing to their petite daughter's every whim and wish.

Eleven-year-old Ashanti wears only first-run designer fashions while her hardworking mother buys her own professional wardrobe at outlet and discount stores. Ashanti thinks in terms of outfits, so her frequent shopping sprees include "necessities" such as matching footwear, jewelry, and even makeup.

Four-year-old Clark, though he is a strong, healthy, and athletic boy, likes to be carried by his mother—everywhere and all the time. When Clark's mother needs to do something or her arms get tired, Clark screams as if the ground were made of hot coals. In many ways, Clark's mother treats Clark as if he were still an infant.

Last but not least, the third grader Devin insists on not only what he wants but also what everyone should want. Devin serves as uninvited consultant to all of his parents' decisions: the color laptop his mother bought, the car options his father chose, the restaurants the family eats at, the movies they see, and the driving routes his parents take.

For thirty years now, as a psychologist working with children and families, I have heard and seen the stress, misery, annoyance, and inconvenience of spoiled children. More so, I have been called in when the fallout of that indulgence has begun to surface or take hold, when children have become impossible to live with or have grown constantly unhappy and insatiable. Frequently, I've entered the scene after many years or even a decade of overindulgence, when parents bring in their malcontented teens who are unable to manage the trials and tasks of growing up toward adulthood. And often I've found that, whatever the child's and the family's issues, parents' straightening out their indulgent parenting has helped to improve everything.

I've written this book with one simple and clear mission: to help parents unspoil their spoiled children. Though the book can help parents to remedy overindulged adolescents, it is aimed squarely at parents of young children, ages two to twelve years old. My method is based on what parents have taught me, over thirty years of clinical experience, about raising children who are contented, happy, and fulfilled. There's little virtue in reinventing your own parenting wheel. Why shouldn't you and your child profit and learn from other parents' missteps, trials, and errors?

But, as we all know, there are plenty of good books out there already on child rearing, discipline, and raising children with moral character. Why another one, and why this one?

Traditional books on parenting are long, dense, and require parents to read through many substantive chapters of background and theory before getting to the punch line, a final chapter of advice. As a parent of grown children, I recall the exhaustion, confusion, and frustration. The parents of young children I know are overworked and overextended. A majority of the single parents I know are even more overworked and overextended. The parents who need this kind of book have the least time, energy, and attention to read books about parenting or anything else.

And so I have aspired to write a book that presents what's important in a format that goes down fast and easy. The strategies of this book are clear and doable—they are based on a solid and deep understanding of children and parents. While the method works quickly, it in no way represents fast-food-style parenting. In addition to improving home life, the methods herein can transform children's insides, promoting their capability and resilience in handling life today and tomorrow.

The book itself consists of twenty-seven chapters that, step by step, help parents build "unspoiling" attitudes and behaviors. Each chapter centers on a short anecdote, case study, or idea that aims to make its points vivid, tangible, and memorable. Chapters include tips and strategies that translate these points to real life and real unspoiling. Early chapters offer a process to quickly reestablish and extend parents' place in the family and at home. Later chapters focus on the best parenting practices to handle common issues that arise during unspoiling, like discipline, unspoiling in public, and unspoiling yourself. The sum of these chapters will, I hope and trust, remind mothers and fathers of their own powers, thereby transforming their parenting from spoiling to its opposite. Each and every chapter, from the get-go, is designed to move you closer to unspoiling parenting and an unspoiled child.

As the adage goes, an ounce of prevention is worth a pound of cure. A few lucky parents will read this before they have gone down a harder road. They will have little to retrace and amend. The book will be a guide to continuing their constructive ways.

The good news is that, for the rest of you, those who've already slipped into a spoiling routine, there is plenty of time to make it right. It's not too late. Start this book and its methods today, and before you know it, your child and family will be looking more like you'd once imagined them. And soon enough, when you peek in the mirror, you'll be looking a little more like the parent you want to be.

In spite of the seven thousand books of expert advice, the right way to discipline a child is still a mystery to most fathers and...mothers. Only your grandmother and Genghis Khan know how to do it.

—BILL COSBY

1. Admit It

DOES ANY OF THIS SOUND FAMILIAR? Your child whines, demands, and complains endlessly. He screams at the mall, throws tantrums in the restaurant, and holds his breath at home until he turns blue or, if he's unlucky, until he gets his way. He shows little gratitude for what you do and seems to take it all for granted, ever asking for more.

"What have you done for me lately?" is his mantra. No matter how much you do, he notices only what you haven't done for him in the last few minutes or hours. At the slightest frustration, he tells you how bad you are, or how he's certain that you don't love him. You do almost everything for him, but he is loath to do anything in return and leaves you to battle for an ounce of cooperation.

Your words or instructions seldom suffice to enlist your child's obedience. He pushes for repeated explanations, accuses you of being unfair, and argues his point like some pint-sized lawyer until, unable to take it one more second, you surrender and buy one more toy, let one more bedtime go, abandon one more limit.

If you live with all or even some of this, your child may be spoiled. But you need me to tell you that like you need another credit card. You've probably known it yourself for months, maybe years. Better than anyone, you know what you've been doing and what life at home has been like. Unfortunately, and for all sorts of reasons, you just haven't been able to remedy the problem.

One thing is sure: your inability to do something about it is not because of a lack of love or caring. Your child's spoiled behavior matters to you a lot, and not just because of the way it stresses you out and torments you. As much as your child frustrates you and wears you out, your concerns go far beyond what it's like to live under her tyranny.

You fear the consequences for your indulged child. You worry about what her being spoiled means for her well-being not just at home but also on the playground and at school. You may fear for her future, knowing that some spoiled children can grow into spoiled adults unable to assume and manage the restraints, hardships, and responsibilities of adulthood. You realize that overindulged children may be prone to anxiety, depression, and troubled relationships. And you recognize that spoiled children risk developing skin that's too brittle to defend them against the arrows and insults that life will fling their way. You are not alone—these concerns are extremely common.

Everyone—parents, grandparents, educators, clergy, and mental health professionals—agrees that children need love and discipline. And children need to learn to cope with life if they are to thrive. They need to learn patience and humility. They need to learn how to manage failure, to own their mistakes and fix them, to see their misdeeds and make sincere amends, and so on. Most parents could think of many more of these childhood can't-live-withouts.

But it won't surprise you to hear me say that a child's healthy and moral psyche doesn't usually pop up out of the blue. Nor will love single-handedly save the day. Growing up without discipline puts a burden on children.

Everyone—parents, grandparents, educators, clergy, and mental health professionals— agrees that children need love and discipline.

Without a parent's gentle and firm guidance, children are at peril of growing into immature and selfish malcontents who can never be satisfied and who view themselves as being above the laws of human consideration and respect. They can grow intolerant for the many parts of life that are tedious, unspectacular, and require hard work or perseverance. At its worst, children who never have to toe the line or obey the law are prone to bigger problems with substance abuse, the police, and who knows what else. These are all unsurprising, but you might not know that overindulgence can have other unintended consequences, such as making children more anxious or angry over their being left in charge.

To best understand the approach I am about to lay out, we need to briefly revisit the self-esteem movement of the previous generation of child experts. By this view, parents were advised to actively build their child's self-esteem with unrelenting admiration and positive regard. If criticism and neglect were the enemies of self-esteem, then their opposites—attention and reward—were the antidote. And so, wanting their children to grow up with good self-images and confidence, parents who followed this movement put their all into the task—the more, the better—devoting themselves to the constant provision of encouraging comments, endless compliments and flattery, and a stream of awards and rewards for the most minimal of efforts or achievement. This unwitting and well-intentioned collaboration of parent and expert strove to make children's lives ever rewarding. But by parenting in a way designed to bring only smiles and laughter, parents created precisely what they'd aspired to avoid: children with paper-thin self-esteem who haplessly rely on others and the outside world to provide stimulation, satisfaction, happiness, and most sadly, purpose. Unfortunately, at the day's end, it was the parents themselves who felt that they'd failed their children.

Picture yourself parenting at your best. Does it look indulgent, or otherwise?

But, as is basic to the human condition, we can do only our best and learn from our mistakes. The parenting community now solidly understands that robust self-regard doesn't grow out of continuous flattery and undeserved trophies. It grows out of competency, out of a child's knowing he can handle life, with its deprivations, frustrations, limits, and such. A child needs boundaries and structure to grow and will seek them out when they are absent. A child who perpetually pesters her parents is still searching for the limits she needs to grow straight. Her demanding and disruptive behavior is, to a great degree, meant to test you, to find out what outrageous action will finally get you to react—constructively. Deep down inside,

A child who perpetually pesters her parents is still searching for the limits she needs to grow straight.

your child wants firmer parenting. Though her words may scream for indulgent parenting, her inner self wants something better. And you are about to start giving it.

But before you do, look at the following checklist to see how many of these spoiling symptoms apply to your home:

___Your child ignores you.

___Your child treats you poorly.

___You rationalize your child's behavior.

___You rescue your child from consequences.

___You do your child's chores or schoolwork.

___You yell and nag.

___You speak harshly and hurtfully.

___You cajole and buy every bit of cooperation.

___You make idle threats.

___You explain yourself repeatedly.

___You can't say no.

___You fear displeasing your child.

___You feel like a terrible parent.

___You sometimes forget what you like about being a parent.

And as you get good and ready to begin unspoiling your child, here are a few quick things to try: Be a social critic. Go to the mall or park and let yourself critique or admire the parenting you see. Envision what your unindulged parenting at home might look and feel like. Be hopeful about the future.

When someone starts to criticize your parenting or children, cut them off and say, "This is something I want to work on too."

Anyone who thinks the art of conversation is dead
ought to tell a child to go to bed.

—ROBERT GALLAGHER

2. Commit

IT WAS DIFFERENT BACK THEN.

When my friends and I were children, our parents didn't buy us snacks on the way home from school or on every errand. They knew that, despite our moans, we weren't starving to death. On the rare occasions that we went out to eat, our parents set limits on what we could choose from the menu. Our parents didn't worry about whether we'd had fun at our friend's house, and they didn't conduct post-game interviews to assess whether we'd had a satisfying time at the ballpark. My friends and I saved up our allowances and later our earnings to buy the things we wanted—skates, baseball gloves, stereos, albums, even clothing—instead of having them handed to us. Parents tended not to work second jobs as chauffeurs; rather, they let their children get around town by foot and bicycle and, by the time we were twelve, bus and subway.

We spent little time asking and pleading for things, for there was no point to it. Why bark up a tree when there are no squirrels to be had? By the time we were adolescents, we saw the responsibility for our work, success, fun, and purchases as our own. Instead of plotting ways to get our parents to buy us something, we spent time thinking of jobs or schemes by which we might earn and save to get what we wanted.

It felt good and liberating, and it made us wiser consumers. A child learns to spend more slowly when he's earned his money by his own hands and sweat. Not only did we appreciate the little we got, we appreciated the chance to earn money, mowing a lawn or painting a fence, and then, in turn, we appreciated being allowed to use our earnings to buy something.

While we each give our own parents all the credit in the world, they probably don't deserve quite as much credit as we give them for what I'll call their underindulgent parenting. Advertising had not yet taken over our existence. Choice was an infinitesimal fraction of what it is today. Once when parents bought their kids sneakers, the choice was white or black. The pressure to keep up with the Joneses not only was manageable but also was often a force that supported parents maintaining the "status no." Many parents could comfortably deny their children because they knew, at that very moment, that other parents were doing the same thing right down the street.

Think about it. Could the majority of yesterday's parents have been good parents, and yet a majority of today's parents be not-so-good parents? That just can't be. Parents are parents, and they have been forever. Or to paraphrase an adage that's been used by many, "Parents are not as perfect as they used to be, and they never were." We can't turn back the clock, and there are many reasons we wouldn't want to. And yet how can there not

> *"Parents are not as perfect as they used to be, and they never were."*

11

be lessons for us to take from the history of parenting that came before us?

What are those lessons? A child learns gratitude by not getting everything she wants. A child learns patience by waiting. A child learns generosity by sharing and giving. A child learns self-control by having to control herself. And above all, she learns contentment by not being trained to always need more and faster.

We are all products of our past, our times, and our society. To some degree, it doesn't matter what came before or what will come fifty years into the future. In fact, history suggests that even Socrates and the ancient Greeks complained about the growing problem of spoiled children. According to an Egyptian manuscript at Oxford University, a boy angry that his father went to Alexandria without him demanded a gift of a lyre and threatened to stop eating and drinking. Like the parents who've come before, all you can do is do your best from this moment on. Commit to unspoiling your child, and your child will follow.

As you are about to embark on your program of unspoiling, start shaking up how you think about your child. For example, some parents research camps, music teachers, and vacations as if their children's futures were hanging in the balance. Try to find greater balance while making decisions on your child's behalf.

Make this book and its method a priority for seven days. Just seven. Do your best to follow the strategies. Then judge for yourself where that takes you and your child. Pledge to yourself that you will not, under any circumstances, explain away your child's behavior as being due to soda, a lack of naps, or the rainy weather. You will see your child and his behaviors more clearly, and own that they have something to do with your parenting. Don't let anything deter or distract you from your commitment. Not bowling night, a cold, or a late night of work will detract from your focus on

Commit to unspoiling your child, and your child will follow.

unspoiling and this method. Your commitment is about to take reign.

After seven days, there will be work left to do and progress to achieve. But you will know more surely and confidently how your unspoiling campaign will go and what to expect. You will be solidly on your way. By that time, your successes and insights should inspire you to keep on with the method and your unspoiling. And, as you'll read next, you will change your attitude to become more authoritative, a parenting approach that you can grow to feel comfortable with and proud of.

> Know from the get-go that in your effort to unspoil, you will slip. Don't start hating yourself. Just get back on track.

The child supplies the power
but the parents have to do the steering.

—BENJAMIN SPOCK

3. Level the Playing Field

I THINK IT'S FAIR TO SAY THAT, at least in the eyes of the child, spoiling parents have lost some of their authoritative presence. What Diana Baumrind wrote almost fifty years ago is just as true today: authoritative parenting is parenting that is both responsive and demanding (from her classic, "Effects of Authoritative Control on Child Behavior" published in the journal *Child Development* in 1966). Authoritative parents hold clear expectations and set firm limits even as they do all of that good and necessary nurturing, respecting, admiring, affirming, and such. Authoritative parents seek and work to foster children's capacities for both self-determination and conformity, to be themselves even as they fit in and belong (to a society, community, home, and later workplace).

Baumrind contrasted authoritative parenting with two other styles: authoritarian and permissive. Authoritarian parenting, as the name sounds, makes the child's obedience the highest priority. Raising the child to comply with the rules and norms—of the law, society, school, home—leads the parents' way in their actions and decisions. Children are taught to obey and not to question, even if the rules appear or actually are unreasonable or arbitrary. Although these children often grow up to be rule-abiding citizens and good students, Baumrind found that they suffered in important ways. They tended to be anxious and withdrawn. They lack an inner strength to believe in their own perceptions and convictions, to think for themselves, and to make independent moral choices.

But Baumrind found that, when compared to what happens in authoritarian homes, children raised by permissive parents were prone to fare worse, much worse. The children of overly permissive parents were unable to regulate their emotions. They rebelled and defied authority, and they displayed antisocial behavior, meaning that they disobeyed rules and seemed to consider themselves above the laws of human and mutual consideration. Also of note, they tended to give up easily when facing challenges of most any sort, whether academic, interpersonal, or work related. What exactly does the permissive parent do? Baumrind lays it out best:

> *The permissive parent attempts to behave in a nonpunitive, acceptant and affirmative manner towards the child's impulses, desires, and actions. [The parent] consults with [the child] about policy decisions and gives explanations for family rules. She makes few demands for household responsibility and orderly behavior. She presents herself to the child as a resource for him to use as he wishes, not as an ideal for him to emulate, nor as an active agent responsible for shaping or altering his ongoing or future behavior. She allows the child to regulate his own activities as much as possible, avoids the exercise of control, and does not encourage him to obey externally defined standards. She attempts to use reason and manipulation, but not overt power to accomplish her ends (p. 889).*

As you can see, and as you probably know first-hand, being a permissive parent does not equal being a bad parent. Permissive parents are thoroughly kind and loving parents who want nothing more than to raise happy and contented children who grow up to be happy and contented adults, fulfilled in every way. Although their authoritarian counterparts worry about their children misbehaving, permissive parents worry most that they might somehow squash, wound, discourage, or inhibit their child's being.

Children from authoritative homes tend to be livelier, happier, more emotionally self-regulated, resilient, socially adept, and flexible.

You love your children dearly. You just have to learn how to do the stricter stuff better and with some regularity. Learn to do that, and you will quickly grow into an authoritative parent, which developmental research tells us is the healthiest ideal. On average, children from authoritative homes tend to be livelier, happier, more emotionally self-regulated, resilient, socially adept, and flexible. They are able to live in balance between their self-will and the demands of society, and they tend to have confidence in their abilities to make decisions, face difficult tasks, and so on.

I am willing to bet that the ways of an authoritative parent match your ideals of how you'd like to parent. I suspect that, were I to ask you what you want in life, that you would wish nothing more than to do a supremely good job with your children. And if I asked you to rate your priorities in life, raising a thankful, appreciative, considerate, confident child who can work, study, and comfortably assume the life of an adult would be at the top of your list.

If you've picked up this book, odds are that your parenting has strayed from your values. But you are about to bring them back in line, along with your child.

This book and its methods, while focusing on the unspoiling of your child, are all about becoming that authoritative parent. How can you get that transformation off to a fast start? By leveling the playing field.

Children raised by permissive parents were prone to fare worse.

What do I mean by that? I mean that your child, like some crafty old coach, has gradually and stealthily tipped the field, and all its advantages, toward herself. Somehow, as we'll talk more about later, your child has gotten you to forget how to say a no that you really mean. Over days and months (and maybe years) of resistance, your child has gotten you to ask him to "hurry up and pick just one candy bar," and has convinced you to actually feel and believe that you are being tough and insistent. What, in the first place, ever happened to just a plain "no candy bar"? To use a sports analogy, you are going up against your child with a heavier ball, duller skates, and one hand tied behind your back. Is it any wonder you keep losing?

Choose a few words that highlight how you wish to parent from this day on. Write them in a journal, or on an index card, or on the borders around a photo of your child. Peek at your inspirational adjectives at the start, the end, and throughout your unspoiling day.

Although there is plenty you can begin doing, there is also plenty you can stop doing, and these changes will give your unspoiling a turbo boost off the starting line. You can accomplish a lot by stopping the nonsense and by no longer relying on old tricks that, more than anything, have weakened your authority and made you less effective and confident as a parent. The following chapter revisits common parenting strategies you may be using right now, strategies that are prone to go awry, with tips to straighten them out and stop doing the stuff that's not working.

Sketch or download a symbol of your indulging—an ice-cream sundae, toys, television, whatever. Draw a red circle around it with a bold line crossing through it. *Spoiling not allowed.* Put the symbol on a small sign, poster, sticky note, computer wallpaper, or PDA background.

If evolution really works, how come mothers only have two hands?

—ED DUSSAULT

4. Stop the Nonsense

WHEN PARENTS FIND A STRATEGY that works, they tend to use it again and again, ever the same way, even long after it has lost its magic and power, which sooner or later always happens. Parents are especially likely to resort to these tricks when stressed, tired, overwhelmed, or otherwise feeling helpless and unsure of anything better to do. But these tricks often don't work and can backfire, weakening a parent's voice and effectiveness and fortifying the child's resolve to disobey or persist. The following sections go over some of these frequently used strategies.

Counting to Three

The counting-to-three method can get toddlers to snap to—until, soon enough, they realize they don't have to. Parents say something like, "Don't make me get to three. Or else…" And the child keeps on her merry way, as if the parent had never spoken. *Or what?* I imagine the child asks back. *Or then you'll really be lost as to what to do with me? Or you'll be so frustrated that giving in or hitting me will be your only options? Or you'll have to keep counting to a hundred?*

There's only one way that I have seen that counting to three works, and that is this: as a warning that the child has until the count of three to shape up. If the parent reaches three, then the parent backs up his or her words and doles out a negative consequence to the child. In other words, counting to three works when parents use it not as a trick but as a tool tied to clear, purposeful, and authoritative parenting. If you use this strategy properly and enforce it, your child will know to behave. Children won't want to experience the negative consequence. Also, you will find that you're not afraid to count right to three and that you have no need for ever-growing fractions between two and three. (For more elaborate applications of this method, you might get a copy of Thomas Phelan's bestselling *1-2-3 Magic*.)

> When you find yourself wanting to call your child a spoiled brat, stop for a moment and wonder how she got that way. Is it her fault or someone else's?

Time-Outs

Time-outs are a mixed bag. They can provide children and parents with valuable space to separate and cool down. When used briefly and wisely, time-outs can help children regroup. When used inconsistently, indiscriminately, and in moments of confusion or frustration (for either a child or a parent), time-outs can leave young children feeling abandoned and ashamed, like those turn-of-the-century children sitting in the corner wearing a dunce cap. But my experience has shown me that the time-out has become many parents' singular weapon. A young child can reflect on what he did for only so long, usually a handful of minutes. Like genies left for centuries in a bottle, children who spend too much time in time-outs risk growing mostly angry and vengeful.

If you find that time-outs sometimes work for your child, use them judiciously and in situations or contexts that make sense to you. Such contexts involve circumstances in which it is likely that your child can use the time-out to think, cool down, and regroup. Short, well-defined, and occasional time-outs are sure to work better than longer, vaguer, and more frequent time-outs. But even less defined time-outs are better than destructive battles that end in hitting or mean words. After all, you never want to corner your child to the point where she has no choice but to strike out or run. When you see your child growing overwhelmed, it's time to back off. Nothing good comes from pushing a child to the brink.

Promising

"But you promised!"

We adore our children and want to give them everything. We want to promise them the moon even though we know that we'll never be able to give it to them. But what does it feel like to be repeatedly promised what is never delivered? And where does that leave you, the promiser? Your reputation will precede you. You will disappoint. And you will be accused. "Liar!"

You can promise as much as you'd like to always love your child. That's one request you know you can keep! But ask yourself why she needs you to promise what you'll buy her tomorrow or where you'll take her or whether you'll be home when you say you will. Maybe you have a bigger problem to take care of. Why do you make promises when what you really mean to say is "No," or "We'll see," or "I'm not deciding now"? Why do you make promises when you know there's a good chance you will break them?

So what do you say when your child asks you to promise that you'll take him to the park tomor-

But ask yourself why your child needs you to promise what you'll buy her or where you'll take her.

row? How about, "I plan on taking you to the park tomorrow"? That should be plenty, unless, of course, you don't regularly come through or you usually come late or not at all (that's a bigger issue that you'll want to rectify and address). Or what if your child asks you to promise that no one, not even the beloved family pet, will ever die or get sick? False reassurance can make you feel better in the moment, but it doesn't really reassure in the long run. Difficult questions like this require honest and thoughtful answers, such as, "I wish I could promise you that, sweetie. But all living things, including people, die someday."

Think about what you're saying, and promise only things you can deliver on.

Dealing

"Do you want to put on the blue or the green pajamas?"

Rather than struggle over every one of the countless moments in a toddler's day, parents often use this clever notion of choices. Parents offer two choices that they can live with—in this case, blue pajamas or green pajamas. The concept isn't bad. It has the potential to achieve two important goals: (1) getting what you want (your child in bedclothes) and (2) giving your child some of what she wants (doing it her way).

This device works like a charm. Until, being creatures of (bad) habit, parents overdo it. When a parent says, "Do you want to put on the blue or the green pajamas?" the parent means, "You are putting on pajamas, so which ones do you choose?" But often the child hears, "Do you want to put on pajamas now, later, or not at all? It's up to you."

If parents rely too much on this linguistic strategy, they lose their muscle for making decisions and exercising authority. They risk getting so used to asking that they forget how to just state a demand. "Let's get going" devolves to "Shall we get going?" Asking a four-year-old whether he wants to go to child care today doesn't make sense when you have to be at work in an hour. Especially when you know he'd prefer to stay home.

Giving clear, explicit instructions goes hand in hand with offering a choice. By the end of this book, you'll be able to simply tell your child that she needs to get into her clothes pronto—and she will.

Rewarding Whining and Demanding Behavior

Anyone who has ever been anywhere in public can readily attest that children whine, scream, and push for what they want. And it often works. But there is no surer route to spoiling than by a parent's reinforcing such undesirable behavior. Every parent knows this as well as any child psychologist does. And no parent wants to raise a child who is obnoxious. So why do parents give in? Often because they feel trapped, stuck, or at a loss for any other way to cope.

It can be the toughest thing in the world to do, but if you try not to surrender to any voice or gesture or behavior that feels like whining, you'll move forward. Try saying something like, "I'll be able to hear you better when you talk in a regular voice." Children hate not being listened to. Calmly and firmly wait, and the odds are that your child will tone down, fast.

"That's Inappropriate."

This phrase is not my favorite. *Inappropriate* is a big and odd word, especially to use with a child. I think kids tend to turn off when hearing it. And to other adults, it usually means something sexual, though not always. Plus it seems kind of detached and clinical. Why not use plain English when it works better? Instead of telling your child that something he says or does is inappropriate, try saying something more direct. "There's better ways to express that." "It's not OK to do that."

"I don't like that." And so forth. Be clear and explicit in your language.

Idle Threats

Idle hands may be the devil's workshop, but when it comes to parenting, they are nothing compared to idle threats. The dilemma is, How do you make a threat that's not idle?

It's hard. Parents make threats the way that they chew gum—that is, without a thought. To paraphrase a wonderful cartoon by Gary Larson, a parent says, "Jacob, if you throw one more paper clip you are going to be sorry. Jacob, I am not kidding. You will lose your dessert and go to bed early. And, there'll be no trip to the video store tomorrow. You're laughing but I'm not kidding, Jacob." The child hears, "Jacob…yadda yadda yadda…Jacob…yadda yadda yadda…Jacob."

A more insidious version of this is when parents show they don't mean the threat while they're making it. "Ella, pick up your toys, or I'll take them away for a day," says the parent, even as he's starting to pick up the toys himself and his surrendering, nonverbal gestures say to the child, "Run, run, go play!"

How can parents transform their threats into something meaningful? Just like with counting to three, you need to back up your words with consequences. Don't threaten something you don't want to take away. It's best not to tell children that their behavior will lose them a trip to the zoo if, in fact, it won't. If you threaten to take away any blocks that are not picked up in ten minutes, you had best be ready to pack up those blocks. (We deal with this common and difficult problem in chapter 8.)

Bribing

As a parent, I know that bribery happens, and sometimes it seems a necessity or a good solution. In general, though, bribery is a strategy laden with pitfalls. Pay him to brush his teeth today, and why will he ever brush them in the future for free? He won't. Buy her a $60 video game for doing a week's worth of homework, and how will she ever find her own internal motivation for doing homework? She won't.

Bribery comes with great costs. It makes today a bit easier; it makes tomorrow a lot harder. Bribery weakens parents' authority and makes them look impotent. With bribery, children think that maybe they can get you to bribe them for many other things that they used to assume they had to do for free. And bribery can be slimy. Grease the kids' palms now, and the slope grows greasier and more slippery. Parents can soon find that, for all intents and purposes, their children own them and that they, the parents, literally must pay for all and any cooperation.

When is bribery a good option? In extreme times. Times when a child's safety hangs in the balance, like when he is 150 feet up in a tree and refusing to come down. Or when she has locked herself into a room and is threatening something worrisome. Or when he has to get through a painful medical procedure. Just don't water down your definition of *extreme* to mean "whenever my child is not willing to listen or obey."

***

The circumstances and dilemmas in which parents find themselves relying on parenting strategies and tricks are so common, relevant, and hard to overcome that we return to them as the book goes on. But you can get a head start by working at more effective ways to implement these strategies.

You have begun to change. It is your new parenting behavior and actions, more than your words, that an-nounce to your child that things are changing, that you're evolving, that a new parenting order has taken the stage. The next chapter shows you how to put that headline into the spotlight—big time. Brace yourself.

> *It is your new parenting behavior and actions, more than your words, that announce to your child that things are changing.*

The more varied and flexible your parenting strategies and tools are, the more effective each will be. Try not to rely on any one trick or tactic.

The quickest way for a parent to get a child's attention is to sit down and look comfortable.

—LANE OLINGHOUSE

5. Grab Their Attention

IN YOUR OWN HEAD AND HEART, you have decided to override the spoiling status quo. You have started to level the playing field by decreasing your reliance on old tricks that have weakened your authority. You have committed to a vision of a happier and more contented home as firmly as if it were a mandate for better schools or world peace. Now you have to send that clear message to your child.

At this point, most parents want to say something aloud to their child. "But don't we have to announce our intentions?" parents ask. "Don't we need to give the kids fair warning?"

"Let's see," I replied to one parent who was tired of asking her son to brush his teeth. "He's eleven years old, which means you've given him 12 reminders per day times 365 days per year times 8 years. That's more than 35,000 warnings, and about 34,950 more warnings than he deserved and needed."

Your child does not need more reminders.

Not to mention that this child was a bright boy with enough memory to remember 493 species of Pokémon. Your child does not need more reminders.

Although writing a proclamation of unspoiling might be a worthwhile exercise for you, there's no need to show or read it to your child. Nor do you need to stand on a milk crate and declare your war on childhood indulgence and entitlement to the family. Haven't loud voices and verbal threats proved their futility?

More warnings not only are not necessary but also can invite your child to not pay attention to you. Your child has probably heard so many warnings

36

that they sound to her like the hum of the refrigerator or the running of the toilet, household sounds that forever run in the background and that she learns to not even notice.

No, as I will say and say again, it will be your actions—not your words—that do the talking and heavy lifting. Your stepping away from parenting tricks that don't help will catch your child's eye. But many children will need something louder and more jarring. For that purpose, and paraphrasing one great president, you need to talk softly and carry a big shtick. By *shtick*, I mean a really good trick up your sleeve, a big deed that, better than any speech or threat, will show your child you mean it, that the party's over.

As a good example, consider Mark. Mark's mom, a lovely woman and good parent, came to me because her son had become a brute. Napoléon who? In laying out just how spoiled he was, she admitted that

Haven't loud voices and verbal threats proved their futility?

for months she'd been taking him to the toy store immediately after his weekly therapy session. "I didn't know any other way to get him here," she said.

We came up with a plan, a plan that both intrigued and frightened Mark's mother. It went like this: She'd leave after Mark's session as if nothing was different. She'd take him to the toy store and buy him his expected reward for having seen me. She'd leave the toy store and head off to run her own errands, just as she'd always done. But when Mark would yell, as he always did, that he didn't want to go with her, and when he demanded that she drive him home that very minute, then, instead of driving him home, she'd turn the car around and drive right back to the toy store. She'd calmly take Mark's toy and bag and walk back in with him to return the item. She'd refrain from yelling or threatening or saying anything as to what she was doing or why.

"His jaw dropped. He couldn't believe it," Mark's mother told me that night by phone. She described how he'd kept yelling at her as they walked all the way across the mall parking lot right into the store. "You can't do this! It's against the law."

Mark's mother felt especially proud that, when asked if there was a problem with the toy, she'd candidly replied that her son had been quite rude and so she wished to bring it back.

The message was not wasted on Mark. He'd been made to see in living color and in one fell swoop that his mother was changing. She'd thrown out of whack all of Mark's expectations and assumptions as to what his mother would tolerate and what she'd never in a hundred years do.

Mark's mother made a grand gesture. That's the point, that it's big and showy. It doesn't really matter exactly what it is. Mark's mother could just as well have returned things that parents seldom think about taking away. Things like sports equipment or back-to-school supplies and clothes. Or she could have targeted a different behavior with her grand gesture, such as Mark's reluctance to brush his teeth, his repeated tardiness to school, his rude behavior in restaurants, his refusal to clean up, and so on.

Any one of these might make a good target for your grand gesture. And why is this grand gesture so important? We'll talk about that more in the next chapter, where we'll draw out plans for some shock-and-awe strategies for common situations with your child.

> Your grand gesture is going to be unexpected, un-characteristic, noisy, in your child's face, strong—and successful.

If your kids are giving you a headache, follow the directions on the aspirin bottle, especially the part that says "keep away from children."

—SUSAN SAVANNAH

6. Shock and Awe Them

WHY IS IT SO IMPORTANT to grab your child's attention? Why can't you just start with simpler and easier steps and work your way up?

In theory, you can. In reality, it's hard to do. Children grow spoiled incrementally, minute by minute, hour by hour, day by day. Your consistently indulgent parenting has gradually and steadily taught your child to look the other way and to ignore your demands. Those countless and tiny, near-imperceptible incidents of spoiling have by now accrued to something large and immovable. Undoing each and every iota of spoiling could take a lifetime. Fortunately, you do not have to do that.

One big and fast action can make children take notice. That grand gesture wows them and throws them off balance. It announces with a sudden bang that you are no longer the parent you were just an hour ago. The beauty is that you needn't waste your breath saying any of that aloud. In fact, to do so might weaken the effect.

One big and fast action can make children take notice.

I think that when parents know they can do such a thing, it grabs their attention, also. Parents often come out of these shock-and-awe moments enthused, surprised, and energized because they went through with it.

As we talked about earlier, when it comes to grabbing your child's attention, warnings are unnecessary and might dilute the sudden shock and awe of your major act of unspoiling. Pronouncing the new you but keeping up the old you will only solidify your child's conviction that you cannot do this. Again, it will be the good unspoiling actions behind your words that show whether there's a new sheriff in town.

By good unspoiling actions, I mean unexpected, uncharacteristic, noisy, strong, and in your child's face. For the intervention of a big action to work, you must take care to create conditions to ensure its success. In the previous chapter, we met Mark and his mother. With my help, Mark's mother chose, as her action, to return a toy she'd bought for him just minutes before. She deliberately picked a problem behavior that repeated itself frequently and that was clear in her mind. The primary objective for you is to pick a behavior or problem that suits the method of shock and awe that you will dole out or to pick a situation in which spoiled behavior generally occurs, even if it is not the problem or behavior that you worry or care about most (we will take care of that problem later).

Here are some typical problems for which you can engineer a shock-and-awe moment. If your child acts up in public, tell her that you are planning on going to her favorite pizza joint on Friday night. Let her and everyone else get excited (but don't let everyone in on the plan, or it will fail). Come Friday night, if you are driving to the pizza place and your child predictably starts to show her spoiled behaviors, *turn around and go home*. If you make it to the restaurant, but your child starts to act up while waiting for the pizza to come, just get up and leave the restaurant with her, head home, and stay there.

This act will work best if your child has not been given the chance, even a minute, to gobble some pizza. And do not take the pizza home. Part of the shock and awe for your child is seeing you do something so unlike yourself and unlike other parents he knows. He may yell that he's starving or inform you that you just cannot leave food that you paid for. If you brought other children with you, don't worry if they haven't had a chance to eat any pizza. They'll survive. And what about the waste of $20 on pizza? That is nothing compared to all of the money you have been wasting on your child. Take it from me, a professional child psychologist—$20 is nothing compared to what therapy costs. (You can apply this strategy just as well when you're going to the movies or on other family outings.)

Do not worry that your firm action will harm your child. It will not.

Is your child ever late to school, or does she dawdle and drive you crazy every morning? Do you have to do all kinds of heroics to get him to school on time? If so, this shock-and-awe strategy might be for you: ask once, and then don't do anything. For example, try asking your child, just once, nicely and patiently, to get ready. Just once! Then go on your merry way doing whatever you do in the morning. When the time to leave has passed, and your child comes yelling that it's your fault, that you didn't do this or that, or that you have to now to do this or that, calmly reply that you had already told him to get ready. Then, depending on your situation, do one of the following:

- Tell your child she will have to go to school late. Calmly refuse her demands that you write a note saying she was sick or something else. Tell her that you will let the teacher know that she was not ready on time. If your child cares about school—and most kids do—she will be furious and upset. If you rescue your child now, you blow it all. Just let the teacher know that you are working on teaching your child to take greater responsibility for getting ready for school and that you expect things to smooth out in a few days. Most teachers are happy to support this kind of strong, proactive parenting.

- Refuse to drive your child to school that day. Let him spend the day being bored at home and worried that he didn't go. This is especially effective for a child who likes school and cares what the teacher thinks. It won't take more than a day or two for him to be ready on time.

  Note: For obvious reasons, do not apply this strategy if your child truly hates school, is afraid of school, or is doing poorly in academics. These types of issues may require professional help.

Another common behavior to address with a grand gesture is poor hygiene. Take toothbrushing as an example. Ask your child to brush her teeth once at bedtime. Then forget it. Your child probably will go to bed not having brushed her teeth. The next day or two, calmly deny her sweets of any kind, whether with a meal or as a snack. Explain to your child that if she doesn't brush her teeth, she can't have sweets. Your

Whatever you do, do not back down.

child may scream that you never warned her. Calmly state that she knows all about toothbrushing and that you hope she makes a better decision next time.

Pulling off a grand gesture is hard. This strategy not only will shock and awe the child but also will shock and awe the parent. Prepare yourself for the parenting act of your life. Plan it out in your head. Write down what you will do, plan it in detail, rehearse it to yourself or with your spouse or partner. Plan it for a day that causes you minimum inconvenience or in which your childcare situation or work or other circumstances permit. Brace for battle. Dress comfortably if it helps. Get up a bit early and psyche yourself. Stay calm; that works best. Remember—it will be your action, not your anger, that delivers the message. And whatever you do, do not back down. In the next chapter, I will flesh out how to stay your ground, and why it works.

If you cave in when carrying out your plan, do not give up. You will try again tomorrow.

No matter how calmly you try to referee, parenting will eventually produce bizarre behavior, and I'm not talking about the kids.

—BILL COSBY

7. Keep Shocking

FROM MY YEARS OF CLINICAL PRACTICE, I know that carrying out an act of shock and awe can be daunting and formidable. "How, though," you may wonder, "does such a single act do its work? What wields its powers? Is it magic or a scam?"

I have now worked with many parents who've marched their spoiled sons and daughters back to the mall or who have performed equivalent grand gestures. My observations, insights, and strategies, however handy and simplistic, are based on an understanding of children that runs deep and is subtle and complex.

When Mark's mom marched back to the toy store with her misbehaving son in tow to return his toy, she carried out a deliberate and well-founded intervention based on sound principles of child development. The mechanics of that intervention are worth exploring briefly.

Carrying out an act of shock and awe can be daunting and formidable.

Instead of returning the toy, Mark's mother could have said things like: "From now on, I'm not going to spoil you." "Starting next week I'm not buying you any more toys just for going to therapy." "You're going to run my errands whether you like it or not." "You have to give me the consideration I deserve, just like I give you."

None of these statements would have been harmful or untrue. But they would have been feeble, and they would have sounded to her son like mealy mush or crumbs to be brushed off his sleeve.

Instead of delivering another idle threat, Mark's mom let her action and its consequences do the talking, all of which defied the laws driving their shared universe.

"You can't do this!" *But I just did*, her steady and quiet actions stated clearly.

"You can't return things you already bought me." *But I just did.*

"You can't betray me like that, telling a strange clerk that I am rude." *But I did.*

"You can't renege on your unspoken promise to bribe me every week." *Ditto*, goes the chorus.

"You owe me, big time." *True, absolutely true. I owe it to you to be the best parent I can be, even when it's hard and potentially embarrassing for me.*

In one swift, powerful move, Mark's mother turned her son's world on its ears, and warned him in the clearest way that he could understand. Because her action spoke loudest, Mark's mother could save her voice and heart for more important matters. She didn't need to scream at her son as she always had. She didn't need to tell him how selfish, inconsiderate, or bad he was. Nor did she need to explain herself and what she'd done. Mark knew why, and in case he didn't, he'd heard what she'd said to the toy store clerk.

But as Mark's mother would have been happy to tell you, her son still tried like mad to blame her. "You stink." "You're a terrible mother." "I hate you." "You lie." "You're mean." "You don't love me"—and maybe the toughest for her to have heard—"I don't love you, and I never did." When a child acts and speaks like this, it's proof that he is desperate and knows the score.

> Your action will throw your child off-balance, but try to stay centered and calm.

With my support and caution, Mark's mom let him rant and rave all he wanted. It shouldn't surprise any parent that Mark eventually promised to do better and begged for another chance to go back to the toy store that afternoon. "I'll run your errands with you," he pleaded. "I'll say thank you and be helpful." But Mark's mother knew not to take his bait, dangerous bait that could have destroyed all her hard work. She knew that Mark would have umpteen chances to behave better—tomorrow and probably every day of his childhood—and not lose his toy. But it wouldn't happen that day.

I'd encouraged Mark's mother to strive to stay calm throughout her shock and awe. Why? Calm enabled her to think clearly, to maintain her position and perspective, and to remember why she'd done this in the first place. By staying calm, she helped to keep the tension and responsibility where it belonged—in the child. As much as Mark made noise and protested to the contrary, as much as he tried to pin the blame on his mother, he knew who was at fault.

Your child will feel loved because you cared enough to take the parenting road less easy.

Because Mark's mother took firm and clear action, and stuck to it, she had no need to show anger. In fact, by the very virtue of what she did, she felt neither frustrated nor angry; she felt effective, satisfied, and proud. Because she'd let the actions carry the day, she did not have to punish Mark with anger or rejection. She was free to empathize with his loss of the toy and his bad choice. Mark's mother felt for the fact that her son had been indulged (by her). Taking action led her to see clearly how spoiling had created hardship for and obstructed the growth of the son she adored. But that clarity and regret, she was starting to realize, did not have to lead to the old, familiar cycle of guilt and leniency. She loved Mark too much to let that happen again.

"I know how disappointed you are," she told him to his surprise. "I know that pretty soon you're going to make better choices." Although Mark appeared to push away his mother's hugs and empathy, it was clear he knew that she felt badly that he had to go through this, just as he felt loved because she'd cared enough to take the parenting road less easy.

> If you see immediate benefit after your action, such as if your child seems more contented or better behaved, take notice. This tells you that you are doing the right thing.

Parents who are afraid to put their foot down
usually have children who step on their toes.

—CHINESE PROVERB

8. Parent 'Em Where It Hurts

I'M NOT TALKING, OF COURSE, about hitting your child. I'm talking about giving your child a consequence that is meaningful to him or her. It can be a new or beloved toy. It can be a trip to the zoo or the bowling alley. It can be a second dessert or even the first one. It can be sweets for a whole day. Sometimes, as in these examples or the examples we talked about in chapter 5, it is fairly obvious what you should take away or, more accurately,

Give your child a consequence that is meaningful to him or her.

what your child should lose. But what should you take away when it is not so clear?

Contemporary life is a technological wonderland. A majority of children spend a good deal of their time playing on computers, video games, iPods, and the rest. Because children value these forms of communication and entertainment so highly and take them for granted, they are often choice objects and activities to be taken away as a consequence for misbehavior.

"That's it!" parents will yell. "You just lost your Nintendo DS for the rest of the day." What do children do? Do they go, tail between their legs, to rue their sad plight in the dark corner of their room? Do they fall into bed and sob over their loss? Without their electronics, do they walk outside to play ball with their friends? Or, bored to death, do they come out to hang out with their parents, offering to help their mother pick up the family room?

Maybe—I suppose that some child somewhere has done one of those things. But what do most children do in this situation? Instead of their handheld video game, they'll play on the family's video game system, a sibling's handheld video game system, or mom's laptop—if they don't go next door to use the neighbor's Gameboy. Over and over in my practice, I have seen parents take away electronics from children who cope by doubling their use of other electronic toys. Take away video games, and they'll play computer games. Take away the computer, and they'll watch movies and television.

Being an unspoiling parent is a lot of work. But it is a small price to pay for an unspoiled child.

To shock and awe that high-tech child, you probably have to hijack his whole electronic load. That brings up a critical point: being an unspoiling parent can be a lot of work. You might have to disconnect and remove a lot of equipment. You might have to manage a child who has little idea how to occupy himself without electronics. But remember that dealing with such issues is a small price to pay to have an unspoiled child.

Here's one way to effectively remove electronics. Consider a scene in which a parent has taken away a child's Xbox video game system. You might think a parent would want to make some noise—you know, angrily ripping the plug out of the wall, grabbing the Xbox by one hand, and storming out of the house, kind of like throwing the television out the window. But I'd do it differently. In the evening, when the child has fallen asleep, I'd quietly move the game system to a safe place. You don't have to be sneaky and don't fear that your child will find out. Doing it at night makes the removal unceremonious and not in the child's face. The aim is to avoid a major confrontation, which will do more harm than good. You're not trying to humiliate or overpower the child, or to set up a situation in which you end up playing tug-of-war with the Xbox.

The next morning or afternoon, when the child goes to play with the Xbox, it won't be there. "Where's my Xbox?" she'll cry. You'll tell her it is gone for now and that you'll return it in a week. Your child may scream, protest, and tell you why you can't do this to her. "It's mine," she'll yell. Or, she'll fall apart and wail, "You don't love me!" You will calmly explain that it is gone, and that you hope, upon its return, that your child makes better decisions or avoids the same misbehaviors so as not to lose it again.

The more highly valued the thing is that's taken away, the more powerful the learning effect on the child. A child, for example, won't willingly lose too many birthday parties.

Let's say your child loves her soccer team, going to practice, and playing in games. But you feel that her spoiled behavior is out of control, and she frequently refuses to do what you ask. For one day, keep track of every time she refuses to obey. Then, when it comes time to take her to the next practice or game, refuse. Tell her that because she did not obey you, she has not earned the privilege of attending her events.

When I suggest to parents the possibility of withholding a sports activity from their child, many recoil. "But getting outside is good for her." "What will I tell her coach?" "Oh, great. She'll get exactly what she wants. She hates swim practice." Sounds like a confusing mess. But confusing messes can and need to be sorted through, teased apart, and straightened out.

If your child will be thrilled to miss the sport, then withholding the activity is not a good shock-and-awe strategy. Keep looking. If your child wants to go, however, this may be your big opportunity. Tell the coach you are working on some issues with your child. The coach is probably a parent, too. If you and your child both feel that your child will be letting the team down by not participating, then that's all the more reason not to drive him to practice. It is obviously something he cares about. If you feel that the team needs your child for a game, then delay the consequence and keep him from going to the next practice or two after that game. Be creative.

You can use the same reasoning to devise consequences involving dance rehearsals, music lessons, and birthday parties—anything that is meaningful to your child and for which the loss will resonate.

Tantrums

It won't surprise you that many children will resist and fight parents who are taking away what they want. They will throw mighty tantrums. Do not fear, and do not surrender. For all of their noise and combustion, tantrums are often a part of a healthy childhood. They are not in themselves indicators of illness, disturbance, or wayward parenting. Strive to see tantrums as serving an important function for your child, allowing her to vent some frustration or anger or helping her to reset her emotional equilibrium. Neither punish nor criticize your child's tantrums. Instead, work to accept and understand them.

What can parents do otherwise to help their child during or after a tantrum? Help your child learn to recognize growing distress, and support her by expressing yourself in words. Be a good listener. See your child's escalating noise and behavior as an appeal for help with mounting distress. When your child starts to make unreasonable demands, stand firm. Do not threaten, and do not match her anger with your own. Let your child know that you get her frustration and that you care. Once the tantrum crosses the no-return mark, do not try to stop it. This is not the time to reason with or give a good talking to your child. She is in no mood or state to figure things out. After the tantrum, allow yourself to be kind, accepting, supportive, and appreciative of your child's reactions to what happened. Beware of dissecting the tantrum. Your child likely wants to just get past it. See what you can learn from the tantrum to help both you and your child from now on.

You've caught your child's attention, and now she will be watching you closely. Let's say she went ballistic and threw a terrible tantrum at first but then afterward turned into the best little girl she's been in a long time. She probably felt safe and sound in your sturdy and firm presence. "Was that glorious and unspoiling parenting moment a fluke?" she will wonder, "Or is that really my parent?"

It is all too easy to lose your child's attention. How? By giving in. By feeling so bad that you go back to the store and buy the toy, or by making a deal to buy it if your child is good for the rest of the day. Mistake! The toy, event, or privilege is gone—period. You both have to accept this if you are going to get anywhere. If you renege on the consequence, you will have done worse than sabotaged your efforts. You'll have taught your child how to ignore and wiggle past even your shock and awe, your most spectacular act of unspoiling.

So what's next? In a day or two, do another shock and awe. Don't rush into it, though. Lay it out ahead of time, like you did the first one. Design it so that it is sure to work as well as or better than your first one did. If your first grand gesture didn't work or if you sense that your problems are bigger than the ones we've discussed here, then read on.

> Tantrums should become less frequent as you proceed through unspoiling. However, they might become more intense for a short while.

Never raise your hand to your kids.
It leaves your groin unprotected.

—RED BUTTONS

9. Establish End Stops

I ONCE CONSULTED WITH SADIE, a mother who'd brought her son for treatment because she couldn't handle him. When Sadie got up to clean the mess that her son, Sean, had made in my office, he stole her seat in a big armchair across from me. Sadie didn't try to reclaim her seat. Without a word or glance, she sat down in a small chair off to the side. When I asked her about it, Sadie said she didn't care where she sat. But we soon learned that she'd kept quiet out of fear that Sean would have started a battle and won. I witnessed firsthand the reason that Sadie had come for help: she had no control over her child, and neither did anyone at school or anywhere else.

In some families, "parents without control" might refer to nothing beyond a child's routine posing of small challenges to her parents' requests. But in some families, like Sadie's, parents without control can be sowing the seeds for a child who will do whatever he wants whenever he wants. Such a child can grow defiant, aggressive, delinquent, and so on.

Parents like Sadie walk on eggshells around their children, forever talking and wrangling, deceiving themselves into believing that they're in charge. Thus handcuffed, parents are prone to look the other way and not even try to set limits, lest the child overrun them, forcing parents to face their frightening impotency.

> *Parents walk on eggshells around their children, forever talking and wrangling, deceiving themselves into believing that they're in charge.*

To establish any kind of authoritative parenting, there has to be some place where you can dependably draw a line in the sand that your child just won't cross. I call such a line an end stop. An end stop is a critical point at which both the parent and child know that the child will not dare cross, push farther, defy, or in any other way transgress one more inch. I've borrowed the term from poetry, where it refers to a grammatical stop, a period. Here, it stands for something solid and unmovable, like a baseball backstop or Jersey barrier that lets nothing through.

What does an end stop look like? It's a parent saying about any limit, "I mean it. Do not test me." And the child, knowing that the parent means what she says, does not go one inch farther. Specifically, the parent might say, "That's it. You have lost the party. You cannot have a party." And the child, knowing that he now really has lost the party, settles down, knowing just as surely that if he pushes on, he will lose the whole birthday weekend. The child who knows his parents have sturdy end stops will not have to push and test to find the limits and boundaries. He knows that they exist, and he knows exactly where!

The child who knows his parents have sturdy end stops most likely has pushed through to them and experienced their force firsthand. She has lost that party, that weekend, that toy, and she knows her parents are not afraid to do it again.

What does an insecure end stop look like? A parent says, "Go ahead, defy me, and that will be the end of soccer for the next two weeks." The child stares, thinks, stammers, and halfheartedly misbehaves, all while studying the parent's response. The parent then says, "Well, you know I won't keep you from soccer, but I'll think of something." The child yawns. The limit has been breached. The child has not experienced the force of firm end stops, so he keeps pushing, never knowing when the barrier will take hold.

If your end stops have been shaky, think about how your child treats end stops in other areas of life. If you have no control over your child at home, and yet she behaves very well at school and in other people's homes, take heart. This is a common situation, and one that is better than many other possibilities.

Your child's ability to regulate behavior in accord with the school (and maybe, other homes) indicates that she does indeed have internal end stops. That she can control herself in other places tells you that you have raised her well enough to comply with the rules and norms of other environments. The most likely explanation for the discrepancy in her behavior at home and school is that the structure and limits of school and other adults are clear. There's less ambiguity and ambivalence on the part of teachers. Your child knows what's expected. Expect the same of your child at home, and you will (eventually) get it.

Parents who have set end stops are empowered by knowing that they have set firm limits. They know that they have a big-enough tool in their parenting toolbox to ultimately exert control over their child or, better yet, to reliably enlist to engage their child's attention and cooperation. End stops give parents an inner confidence, resilience, and comfort with which to widen their parenting repertoire and ensure its success.

It doesn't matter what kinds of limits or consequences parents establish. All that matters is that parents back their words up with action and hold fast. This may sound a bit like the shock-and-awe act that you used to grab the child's attention. But establishing end stops is not so much about grabbing attention, and it's not a one- or two-shot intervention. End stops are consistently set and enforced limits that, when tested, prove as hard and unmoving as a stone wall. Unlike the near-instant power of shock and awe, end stops require that you demonstrate your steadfastness over and over and over, and over again until your child no longer holds any doubt as to your conviction.

End stops are best established when you child is young. If your child develops an ability to handle your saying no when he's young and growing, he'll be able to accept it when he's older and bigger.

If, however, you are the parent of an older child heading in the wrong direction, you and your child can't afford to lose another day. Your work will be tough and the storm you unleash mighty, but keep in mind that, if you give in now, you may eventually find yourself slogging through thicker quicksand with a child who is bigger, badder, and more resistant to renewal.

Begin by asking yourself why your child doesn't take your end stops seriously. Are you choosing consequences that don't sting? Are you consistently lenient? Did you give in quickly or soon after, allowing your child the thing or activity that she supposedly lost? Do you take shortcuts or undermine your action by waging a verbal battle or by indulging your child on one hand while setting a limit with the other?

It is not about perfection, but it is about regularity and consistency, especially for parents who are behind in establishing end stops. It's unreasonable to expect that everything will go smoothly the first time or two. Your goal is to not give up and to stay thoughtful and motivated so that it works a little better each time, until you get it to where you want to be. Yes, this is a lot of work. But it is a lot less work than perpetually dealing with an out-of-control child and the many other people—school principals, police, therapists, and so on—you might find yourself dealing with if you don't get matters with your child in hand.

> Study the actions of others who have better control over your child than you do.

Perhaps it will help if you imagine that you are your child's teacher and your child is the pupil. Be a little more objective and cool headed, a little stricter and more demanding. Show your child that you will not back down, which means that you care. Do not allow a child to hit you, push you, boss you around, or verbally abuse or intimidate you. Doing so is not cute and will soon grow into something that is a lot less cute. If your two-year-old insists on hanging from your earrings when you hold her, put her down that very second. Let her know in no uncertain terms that it hurts and that you will not allow that! If your five-year-old slaps your hand when you go to take something from him, follow through with an immediate, firm, and sustained consequence.

Tighten your child's world. Communicate with the school and integrate what goes on there with what's going on at home. Create limits and consequences for when your child gets into trouble at school so that you are consistent and steadfast.

Take your child's disobedience and bad behavior to heart, wherever it is happening, whether at home, at school, or on the playground. And don't hesitate to use old-fashioned common sense. If your child mistreats you on Saturday morning, why would you ever give her a ride to the mall that afternoon, no less with a $20 bill? It is foolhardy and risky to reward rude, abusive, immoral, or other bad behavior.

And try to assess your circumstances honestly. How serious is your child's behavior? If it involves violence, extreme verbal abuse, complete defiance, illegal behavior, or early signs of what we call sociopathy (which means a lack of conscience, like stealing candy from a young child or taking advantage of less powerful children), you probably need professional help and shouldn't hesitate to seek it out. If you don't know how or where to find such help, consult with your child's teachers, school counselors, doctors, clergy, or other people you trust in the community. Do not delay, for while your child's issues can likely be corrected, they will probably not be outgrown all on their own.

A child who is neglected will act up and do most anything to get noticed by those she loves and depends on.

A quick proviso: Today's parents work harder and do more. Despite all of the technology and affluence that supposedly make our lives easier, many parents have less time for their children. If you sense that your child misbehaves to get your attention because you're busy, preoccupied, or depressed, the solution is not simply to get firmer and clearer. Take action to make more room and time for your child physically and emotionally. A child who is neglected will act up and do most anything to get noticed by those she loves and depends on. That is a healthy reaction for a child who needs more from her parents and should be taken as an indicator that the problem is not the child.

Don't let any shame or ambivalence get in the way of doing what you have to do or finding professional help. Although there is always time to fix spoiling, helping children who are growing violent or totally unreachable is a more urgent matter.

Because of their size, parents may be difficult to discipline properly.

—P. J. O'ROURKE

10. Exercise Discipline

LET'S TALK A LITTLE BIT MORE about end stops and limits, because they're so important to unspoiling your child.

Children need to learn where they end and where others begin. Limits are the foundation for a child's being able to control himself and live harmoniously in a home and community. Consider what limits do:

- They keep the child safe.
- They keep parents, peers, and others safe.
- They keep your home and property safe.

- They make clear to the child what is acceptable and what isn't.
- They show the child that parents can handle her angry and rejecting reactions.
- They lay the foundation for the child to grasp the rules and laws outside of the home—at school, on the playground, and in society.
- They strengthen the child's self-control and patience.
- They teach the child to channel impulses into play and words (rather than destructive anger and violence).
- They show the child that his parents don't fear taking on the duties of a parent.

Limits demonstrate to children that they are separate individuals in a world of people. "No, you can't go through my pocketbook. It's mine!" "That's your brother's cupcake. You have your own," and "No, we're not raising the heat. If you're cold, you can put on a sweater.

Limits are the foundation for a child's being able to control himself and live harmoniously in a home and community.

Everyone else in the family is warm." (Of course, if the child is ill or fatigued, turning up the thermostat might be a moment of good indulgence.)

Limits also include the notion of boundaries and privacy. It is healthy for parents to have privacy in their bedrooms when they choose. Many toddlers have free run of their parents' bedrooms, offices, cell phones, and laptops. (I hate observing parents awkwardly trying to extricate their phones from their child's grasp.) That your limits make your child feel so totally angry and shut out speaks to the heart of the problem. Children need to grow used to handling such reasonable limits without feeling devastated, rejected, and unloved.

And what about your personal space? Why do you want your child with you every minute anyway? Your child needs to learn how, for example, to share a chair and be close without climbing up your blouse or hurting you. Don't wait for your child's groping fingers to grab at your ears or poke your nostrils. Set your child down and say, "You can sit with me, but I don't like being poked. It hurts." Your words and actions will momentarily sting. But when your child tries again, your warm welcome and steadfast limits will soon help him to find a more comfortable place on or near your lap.

> Try to notice what your child can't do versus what he won't do. Strive to target your discipline and unspoiling at behaviors that your child can control but chooses not to.

Indulged children are often undisciplined children. But discipline and punishment, parents should keep in mind, are not the same thing. Disciplining, setting limits and boundaries, and holding expectations are positive forces that work to establish the conditions under which a child can grow to learn and develop greater skills for self-regulation, emotional expression, problem solving, and so forth. It's all about endowing children as the primary agents of their own lives. Punishment is more parents' attempts to control children. But discipline is obviously more effective and to be cultivated. Here are some guidelines for using discipline to prevent and remedy spoiled children.

Discipline fairly. Don't heap all your discipline on one child. Don't rev your child up and then punish him for being wild. Are you a parent who lives life at seventy-five miles per hour and then erupts when your overstimulated child finally gets to you? Watch that your discipline is in line with the crime. Countering your child's snowball with a barrage of cannonballs will anger and hurt your child more than instill anything good in him.

Discipline reasonably. Take ample responsibility for the disciplinary state of your child and home. It is not your child's fault that you don't set adequate limits. It is not her fault that you use a loud voice as your primary parenting tool. Don't discipline because you are frustrated, irritable, or having a bad day. Discipline when there's good reason to.

Discipline clearly. Know what you want. You can't enforce fuzzy limits. State your limits in behavioral terms. "Be good" or "Don't get me upset" is too vague. How about this: "I'd like you to clean up this art project before starting the next." Recall what we noted about teachers, how they talk to their pupils and how their pupils respond. Strive to use words and language that your child readily grasps. Allow your child time to process, and check to make sure that he has understood you.

Discipline individually. Although there are fundamentals of discipline and unspoiling that apply to most children, the specific circumstances, the child's nature and developmental stage, and so forth, might dictate different forms of discipline. One child may need nothing more than a disapproving frown, whereas another child may need more active discipline. One child may learn the first time, whereas her siblings take longer to learn.

Discipline consistently. Consistent discipline means that the same offense, on average, will get the same disciplinary reaction from you, and regularly. Consistent discipline does not require robotic precision. Two parents or caretakers do not have to be in perfect synchrony. Beware of heaping more discipline on in anger, threatening consequences that become impossible to enforce.

Discipline judiciously. Judicious parenting is thoughtful and well reasoned. Judicious parents seek to understand their parenting. They aspire to discipline in ways that are sound, opportune, and effective. Instead of beating themselves up, they seek to learn from their errors and find new possibilities. They aim to make the most of their discipline and avoid that which is useless or harmful.

Discipline compassionately. Compassion is the disciplinary ace up your sleeve. Parents often misbelieve that disciplinary action must be backed up with anger and intimidation. "Now you've done it!" said with a scowl and some heat. Potent limits and consequences don't require parents to pile on the anger. Once you've set and stuck to a limit—and once your rage and hurt have subsided—let your kindness and empathy show.

Discipline forgivingly. Leave room for your child's authentic feelings about having misbehaved and having been disciplined. Let her apologize and make amends. Let your child cry.

Limits and discipline help children be the kind of children that bring out

When children behave better, their parents are more likely to treat them with good feeling, empathy, and respect.

the best in their parents. For when children behave better, their parents are more likely to treat them with good feeling, empathy, and respect.

Ask yourself, is your leniency a matter of principle or something else?

A parent who has never apologized to his children is a monster. If he's always apologizing, his children are monsters.

—MIGNON MCLAUGHLIN

11. Stop Explaining Yourself

YOU'VE ADMITTED YOUR PROBLEM and committed to its solution. You've given up your unhelpful parenting habits and grabbed your child's attention. You've set limits and declared war on spoiling. You mean business, and your child sees that. She now wonders whether you've got the stamina and stomach to keep it up. She won't curl up and give in, though she's curious and a little apprehensive. Your effective first steps were a wake-up

Today's parents tend to be uncomfortable with their authority.

call. Where to now? It's time to adjourn the court, leaving *Law and Order* on television where it belongs.

Today's parents, and I'm no exception, tend to talk with their kids. In many ways, that is a good change from previous generations of parents. Many children openly discuss their dearest experiences and concerns with their parents. That's surely a blessing. But even in conversation, today's parents tend to be uncomfortable with their authority. Instead of telling their child what to do, they ask. Demands become questions, and questions turn into special elections.

Look what "Please hand me that stick" can morph into at the playground:

"Sweetie, may mommy have that stick?"

"Would you like to give mommy that stick?"

"Wouldn't you rather play with this shovel than that nasty old stick?"

The child's behavior says, *No, no, and still no.*

"Can you pretty please give mommy the stick, and then we'll go to the candy store?" *Now we're getting somewhere.*

"That's a good kid. Wait, wait, come back and give me the stick now, or we're not going to go to the candy store." *I want a better deal.*

"If you don't bring it right now, you're only getting one thing at the candy store." *Do you mean one thing or one bag?*

"You're only going to get one bag of one kind of candy." *But I want a whistle pop, too.*

"Then you'd better come give me the stick right this second." *And a gummy snake?*

"Yes!" mother says, "and a gummy snake. What a good girl you are!" *That's more like it.*

You get the point. And you can understand how, over time, parents come to feel resentment, frustration, and impotence. "Damn it! Give me that stick before I…" *Gee*, the child is left wondering, *why didn't you just say you wanted it in the first place?*

So what's the point? It's time to disbar your mini-attorney. From this moment on, you will no longer offer up twenty-six reasons for your child to clean her room. Nor will you explain and explain again why you want the video games shut off.

Children argue their points with their parents much in the same ways that major corporations do. Both seek to delay what seem like inevitable decisions and penalties. As long as your child questions, debates, and opposes bedtime, he guarantees that he stays up. The battle itself is gratifying.

As long as the two of you verbally lock horns, you are engaged in a tangle that really looks like a civil lawsuit. Sue a wrongdoing party, and that party will do everything to draw it out, stopping at nothing that might sap your strength, consume your resources, and undermine your resolve. How long will the party go at you? Until the fifty-ninth minute of the twenty-third hour and then some. Wrongdoers know from experience that they can wear people down. Their aim and hope? That you will tire and fade, and then give up the case or settle. For a guilty party, a settlement represents a victory that allows it to save both face and money.

Your child likewise has little to lose by battling you to the end. If she loses, she has to go to bed, brush her teeth, or clean up her toys. Hey, wait a minute, wasn't that the worst that could happen to her anyway? And what do you risk by allowing her to wrangle with you? Just about everything—sleep, a headache, self-respect, self-esteem, and so on. And what do you get if you win in the end? Nothing more than if you had been able to stick to your rightful case from the get-go.

Every time you do legal-like battle with your child, you empower her willingness to battle on and again. She gets stronger and better at it. Her taste and skill for negotiating will sharpen. And, scariest of all, should you surrender in the final moments after a long trial, she will learn a treacherous lesson (treacherous for you, that is): to never let up when dealing with you. For your child has seen that, in the end, persistence will do you in and she will triumph.

What can you do when your daughter interrogates you? Refuse to play by your child's rules. Who made her judge and jury? Don't answer her questions. Don't explain and explain yourself. Don't justify your parenting to her. Maybe even say (I can't believe I'm saying this), "Because I am the parent, and I said so."

Teachers are experts at this kind of clarity and precision. "Please take out your science books. Open them to page 16. Read from the second paragraph." No ambiguity there, no confusion, no wiggle room. When a teacher says, "I don't want to hear anyone talking," the children know just what they are to do. Can you imagine the chaos if teachers did what most parents do? "Would you like to stop talking soon?" or "Would you rather take out your science books or your drawing books?" And imagine further the chaos if teachers used a coyly inviting voice and body language while announcing their next order. "OK, sweeties, I don't want anyone hanging around my desk." In minutes, teachers' laps would be crawling with children.

Imagine yourself a teacher with your child in your classroom. Try emulating a teacher's clarity, directness, and expectations for an hour or so, and see what happens.

Parents often create a dangerous framework for conversation that becomes completely habitual and automatic. They not only pose everything as a question but also use terms like *honey* and *sweetheart* to soften the blow of everything. "Sweetheart, would you like to come to dinner?" And the child's reaction says, "Actually, I'd prefer that you bring me a five-course dinner down to the basement so that I can keep playing my game without any inconvenience to myself." "OK," the parent says, "I'll bring dinner down." "How about some carrots before your ice cream?" And the child says, "No, just ice cream."

No more asking. No more explaining.

Stop, look, and listen. So much of parenting happens on the go, even when sitting in the house. We parent the way we grab a soda—thinking about and doing three other things at the same time. In the terms of Eastern philosophers, get more mindful about your parenting, especially about how you talk to and with your child.

You have no need to explain yourself, so don't.

You have no need to explain yourself, so don't. Think of it. You're the parent. You're an educated adult who's had sex, backed into a tree while driving a car, and lost money on lottery tickets. Your child hasn't even finished kindergarten. What does she know? Case closed.

> Practice telling your child your expectations and wishes in statements that declare rather than ask.

Ask your child what he wants for dinner
only if he's buying.

—FRAN LEBOWITZ

12. Take Back the Power

WHAT ARE THE GOLDEN RULES for spoiling your child?
Never allow your child to wait more than a few seconds
for anything. You should have picked her up by the time
her arms went vertical. You should have headed for the
kitchen to refill her juice before her glass ran empty. If
she asks you a question, answer her instantly, even if it
means ignoring your spouse. If you can anticipate what
your child wants without her having to ask, better yet.
Such a child should save her energy for more important
duties, like berating you for responding too slowly.

We know there are children who are the bosses of

their household. They reserve the final vote and veto on everything that happens: what the family eats and when, when and with whom the family sleeps, what they watch on television, and where the family goes for dinner. Some children actually dictate where their parents sit at the table and whether their parents can talk to each other. I've heard of young children who have given heeded advice as to what car or home their parents should buy.

Start ruling the roost yourself. Make all the decisions so that there aren't any for your child to make. Think about it—if you show a toddler a house that's a good value and another house with a giant kids bed in the parents' bedroom, which do you think your toddler will pick?

Change the form of government in your house. A perfect democracy doesn't work. Children often don't vote well on their own behalf. Sometimes, parents need to be benevolent dictators who know what is in their child's best interest.

You can engage your child in decisions that make sense for her age and stature, like picking out her outfit for school or choosing a book to read. But learn to distinguish needs from wants and fancies. Train yourself to think of needs in the bigger developmental sense of the word. Your child's starving desire for a snack is a want, however intense. Food and water are physical needs. Learning how to wait patiently—without disintegrating, feeling unloved, or attacking the person your child feels is depriving him—is, as an example, a developmental need, the kind not to be ignored or put off.

It's fine to acknowledge your child's wish to rule: "You wanted us to buy the red car." But do not apologize or make promises for how you will do better to follow his wishes next time or get all torqued out of shape because your child thought you looked better in the brown tweed jacket. Maybe your child can have a special kind of citizen status. One whose opinions can be freely given and heard but who enjoys neither voting nor veto privileges.

You might try leaving your child at home or out of the picture when making big decisions.

Once you've given the car keys to your child, metaphorically, of course, it isn't too late to take them back. Stop treating your child as royalty whose every want must be met. Teach your child to turn demands into polite requests. Let her wait her turn or until it's convenient for you—a third glass of milk is not urgent.

We know there are children who are bosses of their households.

When parents change their ways, the child will follow (probably with some obligatory fuss and protest). Parents should never feel that they are hog-tied to the ways they parented yesterday. Thoughtful parenting demands continual reassessment and adaptation. That your children tell you that you cannot change should tell you something about the ways you need to change.

Take an extreme example. A parent tells an eight-year-old child that she can swim at the quarry with her teenage cousins. After listening to other parents, this parent realizes she made a mistake. It is not only OK but also imperative that the parent let the child know that the decision has been revoked. That's an easy example, but the logic remains. Your child's life doesn't have to be at stake to justify your changing your parenting mind.

I have many times been astonished to hear about an adolescent having repeated car accidents—because of alcohol, speed, and recklessness—only to have the parents keep repairing the car and renewing the insurance, despite sky-high premium penalties. Why not just buy the child a gun? Parents can take the car keys back, literally and metaphorically.

Giving a child age-appropriate power in the family is a good way to teach responsibility if it fits the child developmentally. It's good for a child to take care of his own schoolwork and school responsibilities befitting his abilities and age. For parents to assume those responsibilities deprives the child of experiences that promote confidence, success, and resilience. Likewise, it's good to let a young child wash her own face and, as soon as she's able, go the bathroom on her own. But to be handed the powers of making adult decisions, of being a parent's confidante, or of ensuring the parent's happiness is too much of a burden for a child.

Although a child who is given too much power may

appear to be older than his age, he will suffer and be more immature in other ways, meaning that he won't get a full chance to grow up on his own through childhood. Think of kids raised on their own. They look streetwise and tough and much older than their age, and they may live that way, too. But inside, they are immature in important and unhealthy ways that make them less fit for grown-up life.

To be handed the powers of making adult decisions is too much of a burden for a child.

I know nothing about the reigning Queen Elizabeth's childhood, but I'm willing to bet that she was very much a child who knew her place in the home. Don't our own children deserve parenting no less royal?

Make a list of matters that, in your judgment, your child should have input on and those he should not.

> *The joys of parents are secret,*
> *and so are their grieves and fears.*
>
> —Francis Bacon

13. Overcome Blind Spots

"Loving your kids to death" is an odd expression. But parents know just what it means. Sometimes the love we feel for our children is more than words can capture, more than we can bear. A mother I worked with, Summer, knew that feeling well.

Summer adored her children. Divorced from the children's father, a neglectful and abusive man, Summer wanted to make their lives good. Not wanting her children to be the products of a broken home, she'd stayed with that man for too long. There was nothing Summer wouldn't do for her children. Tired or ill, or with her own work to do, her children's needs came first.

Summer came to my office carrying bags of candy, bakery goods, and toys. She was the kind of mother who rose early to make pancakes shaped like hearts and who often put surprises in the children's lunch boxes. She'd buy them birthday and Christmas gifts that outran her budget. "I couldn't get them a good father," she said. "The least I can do is give them all that I can." It wasn't until her debt got out of hand that Summer was forced to change her ways.

It'd be an easy shot to criticize Summer. It doesn't take Sigmund Freud to figure out that no amount of goodies and toys will make up for a split family. But then again, who among us doesn't know that impulse—the wish to distract our children or give them something to make them smile so they forget what we know or imagine to be their misery?

Many other parents, like Summer, indulge their children in direct reaction to the childhood or parenting they knew. Many parents have told me that they love to say yes, because when they were children, all they heard was no. These parents indulge and give—things, attention, and affection—less out of unconscious resentment and more out of a conscious choice to nourish their children's joy and spirit. They wish to foster in their children the capacities to want, ask, take, and enjoy from life in a way that they, the parents, never could. It's not rare to meet parents who can indulge and spend on their children in a way they would never do for themselves.

Keep in mind that there isn't a parent who doesn't have blind spots or biases in parenting ways that arise from the past. The goal is not to be rid of such blind spots, for they are part of being human. The goal is to know and watch out for them, so that they don't obstruct your parenting.

There are plenty of good reasons parents spoil their children, and these reasons are as varied as children. It's important not to get caught up in matters of self-understanding that can hinder your unspoiling. But if there is something specific that is holding you back, it's in your and your child's best interest to find a remedy if possible. The following paragraphs go over some common reasons for spoiling children that

> *There are plenty of good reasons parents spoil their children, and these reasons are as varied as children.*

parents in my therapy office have talked to me about, along with some simple advice.

I'm too tired. Rest, nap, and make good self-care a higher priority.

I'm not sure what to do. Read books like this and learn. Talk to other parents and seek help from a professional or groups at your church or in the community that focus on positive parenting. Parenting is a skill. Skills can be learned and honed.

I fear my own anger. Continue to think about and better understand the concept of unspoiling. It will make you less angry, as will your growing ability to not spoil. If abusing your child is a concern or is ongoing, get help.

I fear losing my child's love or friendship. You are likely in no risk of losing either your child's love or friendship. Use whatever means or supports that can help you to get over it. Strong parenting usually fortifies a child's attachment and love for the parent.

I use spoiling to rebel against my own parents. Stop it. Use better methods to deal with your feelings or resentments, such as therapy, parenting groups, or sharing your feelings with other parents or friends. Don't sacrifice what your child needs to wage a hollow battle against your own childhood.

I'm preoccupied with work. Parents cannot help working when they are at work. However, if you are a professional who is a workaholic, know that your children pay a heavy price. You manage to make time for everything and everybody at work. Use that same ingenuity and industry to work on your unspoiling and parenting. Recall that old adage about the fact that no one on a deathbed says that his or her only regret is not having spent more time working.

I fear hurting my child's self-esteem. Well, by now you can anticipate me: your indulging is much more likely to cause problems with your child's self-esteem than is any discipline you impose.

I'm going through marital problems. Get help. Your children need you.

I'm a single parent. This is a hard one. Single mothers carry so much on their shoulders. I hesitate to say anything like, "Just do what you have to." Although I cannot tell you how to do it—or where to find more time or greater resources or a third arm—I can say that, in the long run, unspoiling your home will make your home life steadier, easier, and happier.

I feel guilty. Grab your guilt by the horns and put it to better use. Instead of letting it bully you into being an indulger, use your guilt to energize your unspoiling. That's what your children really need. There's no better antidote to guilt than being a good parent.

I take unconscious pleasure in spoiling my child. Some parents feel deep pain and loss over not having been parented in nurturing and giving ways. Their spoiling of their child is a way to offset that hurt. Reflect on it, journal about it, or talk to others or a therapist.

I have a conscious wish to teach my child to enjoy life. Many parents who grew up in strict or ungiving homes want to teach their children how to want, take, and know joy in ways that they, the parents, never learned. This is OK, unless it overgrows into spoiling.

Talking with a therapist or counselor might help you figure out any one of these issues. But you and your child can't afford to wait for insights into your reasons for spoiling, reasons that can run deep and far outside your awareness. You can try psychoanalysis to uncover those reasons, but by the time you get off the couch, your child will be grown up and gone. Your child needs an adjustment that begins soon, like yesterday. Remember that unspoiling is not about dwelling on the past—it's about focusing on your child's future.

And as we've mentioned before, parents have to distinguish between a want and a real need. Children may want a toy or candy very much. Toys and candy, however, are not needs. Children's needs include things like love, stimulation, and care. Children also need things like limits, structure, and expectations. Parents who, in loving their children to extremes, slavishly fulfill their children's wants may inadvertently deny their children's needs.

Unspoiling is not about dwelling on the past—it's about focusing on your child's future.

For instance, if we always buy a child what she asks for, we will deprive her of a developmental need to learn patience and to tolerate the frustration of not always getting her way. If we never frustrate her wish to be held and carried about, we will deprive her of the opportunity to grow more independent and self-fulfilled. If we quickly give him the solution to every problem, we will deny him the need to grow self-sufficient and resilient. In short, we can give children the world and, in doing so, make them unfit to live in it as adults.

That's not to say there's anything wrong with making children feel loved and special, as Summer did by making heart-shaped pancakes and putting special treats in her children's lunch boxes. Children deserve to feel loved, and parenting like that is healthy and wondrous. Such loving attention lets children know that they matter deep down inside, and that is what endows people with a genuine conviction that they count in this world. Parents who bake and make their children's day joyous are to be commended. Summer spoiled her children because she had difficulties not giving to them, even when it ran against her better judgment, even when she was exhausted, and even when it drained her budget. You know in your heart when you're doing too much.

Unspoiling will get easier and easier. You will get better at it and more comfortable with it. Your children will need to test it less and less.

Raising kids is part joy and part guerilla warfare.

—ED ASNER

14. Hold Your Ground

I BET YOU'RE DOING VERY WELL at unspoiling your child. Let's take this quiz to see for sure: You are walking home from the pediatrician's office where your younger child had a checkup. Your slightly older child demands that you stop to browse the local toy store that opened yesterday, saying that she deserves it for having come with you to her brother's appointment. What do you say?

a. "Great idea! We can see what new toys they've brought in since we browsed there yesterday."

b. "Absolutely. You did such a great job waiting five minutes for your brother that you deserve something very special."

c. You check your wallet and say, "OK, I guess. But I only have $40. Are you sure you don't want to wait until I can get more money?"

d. "I was hoping you'd ask."

e. All of the above.

I gave you five outrageously sarcastic answers to make a point. My experience has taught me well that, when it comes to spoiling and unspoiling, backsliding is a major liability. Otherwise competent and intelligent people who happen to have children will work to set all kinds of limits, only to let them slip away. I suspect you can come up with your own right answer for this quiz, something, perhaps, that affirms your child's good behavior while recognizing that it needn't be rewarded with a purchase. Maybe something like this, spoken as you calmly herd your children into the car: "I really appreciate how much effort you made to be a good waiter at the doctor's. After all, it wasn't even your checkup."

Nowhere is follow-through needed more than in your parenting (except bowling, maybe). As we've discussed, like idle hands and minds, idle threats can be dangerous. What do they teach? The obvious—that we talk big and blow a lot of hot air. When we don't follow through, it's as if we type documents that we neglect to save. Without saving our work, it disappears as if it never existed.

Nowhere is follow-through needed more than in your parenting.

If you take away your child's Xbox for seven days, during that week your child will try to earn, cajole, flatter, charm, and intimidate you to gain its early release. He may appear to have learned his lesson. How easy it would be for you to break down and bring it out prematurely. Don't!

Giving in on the fifth or sixth day can teach your child to scratch and claw until the final gasp (and when children are busy clawing, they usually aren't doing much reckoning and reflecting). Think of your child as having committed a crime that carries a minimum sentence of seven days. Seven-day sentences must be served. If your conviction in your child's conviction is certain, her frantic attempts to undo it, however noisy and robust, will seem meager, transparent, and easy to ignore.

And when it's time to bring the game system back, clearly state your expectations from that day on. Your child may judge that she's finally getting back what is rightfully hers. But you can straighten her out on this one. The Xbox is a privilege, and you, as her parent, know what behavior deserves such a reward. And if your child misbehaves in the same way as before, don't hesitate to press the replay button, doing the whole business again, maybe for longer.

Like a general in combat, plan your next attack. Have your mission and goals set in your mind before entering the battle scene.

As you've noticed, I have stayed away from mentioning specific ages or time frames for consequences. It varies. Younger children learn best over shorter time periods, perhaps hours or a day. School-aged children often need lengthier consequences to feel their sting and to reform their attitude. But there are few hard-and-fast rules. Some teens need only a raised eyebrow; some toddlers need a parental version of Alcatraz.

When you do return whatever it was you took away, don't do something special to make it up to your child. You went through all that hardship to provide your child something he needs to grow up well. That was a loving act. You owe your child nothing more. Are you willing to gamble all that away out of your lingering guilt or discomfort over being a parent with authority?

But let's try rethinking the example about leaving the pediatrician. How would you best reward the behavior of waiting properly at the doctor's office? As I have probably said too many times, today's children don't just grow to be impatient, uncooperative, and insistent. Their parents diligently train them to be that way, even if that training is wholly unwitting, unintentional, and undesired (all of which it usually is). Parents have to keep reminding themselves that what they see is their own doing. I say that not to discourage or blame but to underscore, with hope, that what can be created can be uncreated or transformed.

This suggests that we need to rethink how you treat good behavior. Rather than asking what you can do to reward your child's behavior, you might ask, "What can I do to support, nurture, and promote my child's good attitude and effort?" Paying your child off with a treat or prize will feed into the same problem and only sustain the status quo that you wish to change. You see, if your parenting has become somewhat reactive and willy-nilly, it has, from the child's perspective, become a formal behavioral system of a sort in which the child is reinforced for high-priced cooperation. You have basically been giving your child valued tokens at precisely the wrong times, teaching that indulged behaviors are what parents ultimately reward.

So let's change the scenario. Rather than go into the pediatrician's office braced for a difficult child, elevate your expectations and let your child know about them. "I expect that you will wait patiently while we visit the doctor." And if, as happened in the scenario, your child waits well, let him see your pleasure: "I was proud of how hard you worked to help me out at the pediatrician's." "That took even longer than I thought it would. Was it hard being so patient?" Or perhaps say to the sibling who saw the doctor, "I hope you can learn to be as grown-up and patient as your sister."

Following through and establishing a baseline of unspoiling takes more work than does maintaining it. Over the next many days and weeks, your child will need to test you less and less. You will grow more adept at knowing what to do and at innovating your own version of unspoiling. It will become a second-nature part of your perspective and behavior as a parent.

But on those inevitable days when nothing works, when your newfound unspoiling insights and abilities all seem to fail, try not to despair. When you sense that kind of day, go slow or not at all. Maybe put your unspoiling on hold for the rest of the day. Try not to beat yourself up or doubt your progress. Rather than incite an artificial battle, take the time to renew yourself, or at least pull back to cut your losses. There is always tomorrow.

Take the time to renew yourself.

Rather than anticipate circumstances as potential and dreaded disasters, start envisioning them as potential opportunities for success.

Making the decision to have a child is momentous.
It is to decide forever to have your heart
go walking around outside your body.

—ELIZABETH STONE

15. Allow for Natural Consequences

NATURAL CONSEQUENCES ARE JUST what they sound like, consequences that follow naturally, unless there is some unexpected intervention. For example, if it rains, the ground will be wet. You forgot to put in batteries, so the flashlight dies out. When it comes to natural consequences, childhood and adolescence offer a world of endless possibilities:

- A twelve-year-old boy refuses to wear a hat and gloves, so his fingers are cold at the outdoor skating rink.

- An eighth-grade girl doesn't study for her French quiz, so she fails or gets a poor grade.
- Not getting up early enough to prepare for school, a seventh grader leaves in a hurry and forgets his lunch, so he goes without lunch that day.
- A child eats all her popcorn during the coming attractions, and then has to sit through the movie watching everyone else eat the popcorn they've held onto.
- In a rage, a toddler pounds on his new yellow excavating truck with his father's hammer, so the new truck is dented and broken.
- A fifth grader launches his expensive BMX bike off jumps to see how much damage it can take landing on the pavement, until he breaks it.

The key to natural consequences is simple. All parents have to do is not get in the way. Sounds simple, but it isn't. Most parents have a compulsive instinct to save their children from the natural consequences of their actions. I, for example,

When it comes to natural consequences, childhood and adolescence offer a world of endless possibilities.

did plenty of yelling and blaming, but then I'd undo it all by driving over to the school to bring the forgotten lunch, sharing the popcorn that I'd saved, or helping fix the truck or bike.

Although what I did is easy to grasp for parents, it did my children a disservice. My now-grown children would be the first to confirm my tendency to have done this, and they could readily state their wish that I'd done otherwise, that I would have gotten out of their way. What was it about letting my children feel and live with the consequences of their actions that so unnerved me? What was I afraid of? That they'd fail? That it would reflect on me? Or more likely, that they would learn that they can manage much of their life just fine without their father's constant help?

> By not letting your child experience the natural consequences of his actions, you are taking away what might be the primary learning mechanism of life.

Unless children are in danger, strive to let them cope with what they've created. As your child grows older and has run-ins with the outside world, you may want to run alongside him like some bodyguard or guardian angel. We all understand that wish. But then ask yourself, "How can my child grow strong and able unless she learns to handle life?"

Consider a situation in which a child feels criticized by his teacher. My parents would have asked me what I'd done wrong and quickly gone back to what they were doing. That may sound harsh and unresponsive. But in some ways, by not overly involving themselves in my school life, my parents endowed me with a sense of trust that I have the power and means to manage my own life.

What message do slightly disgruntled children get when they watch their parents take their side against a teacher and run to the school with a lawyer in hand? Such action can sabotage children's burgeoning sense of competency and rescue them from their responsibilities. We do their homework. We run interference for them at school. We do their chores and then underwrite trips to the movies anyway. We let them buy

118

toys with next week's allowance and then never ask them to pay us back. We undermine and bad-mouth coaches and other grown-ups on the outside who attempt to hold them accountable. If our goal is to hinder our children from going out into the world responsibly and capably, why don't we just cut off their arms and legs?

Compare natural and unnatural consequences. A child misbehaves in church. The parent comes home and takes away the child's computer games. Although the consequence is a result of the child's action, the connection is not natural, because the parent could just as well have taken away building blocks, a birthday party, or some other privilege. However, a natural consequence is the actual result of the child's action. The child breaks a video game system in frustration, so the natural consequence is that he now has no working video game.

Natural consequences teach well because they make perfect sense in the world and are not punitively imposed from above or out of anger. They accurately reflect how life happens and works. Because parents do not randomly or arbitrarily pick the consequence, there is no intermediary for the child to blame. If no adult were there, the child would suffer the same consequence. The consequence is clearly the child's own doing (or not doing). And the consequence usually is in proportion to the action.

Sometimes it's unrealistic for parents to let a natural consequence run its course. If a two-year-old misplaces her boots, her parents will buy her new ones so that she can go out in the rain and snow without wet feet. If during a tantrum a young child throws a paperweight through his bedroom window, his parents will likely fix the window so as to make his room tight to the weather. If your tween does something to endanger her health, you likely will intervene, as you should. Parents should consider the child's age, developmental level, and context or circumstances. This may mean substituting something unnatural, such as some other kind of consequence for breaking the window.

Parents also need to use their best judgment when natural consequences make sense. For example, a toddler tries her best to hold on to an ice-cream cone. Another child runs by and bumps into her, the cone tips, and the ice cream plops to the ground. Her parents might well choose to replace her cone. But would they do the same for a five-year-old who, despite parents' warnings, wildly runs up a slide whipping his cone around like a lasso?

A hardworking fourth grader struggles to finish a project that's due the next day. He didn't have as much time to work on it as planned because of an infrequent, out-of-town family reunion. While he was rushing to get the project done, he accidentally ruined it. His parents might tell him to get some rest and that they will talk with his teacher to ask for another night to fix it. But would other parents want to do the same for a child who forever blows off schoolwork to watch television and play computer games?

If there is no compelling reason to interfere and rescue, don't. The beauty of natural consequences is that the child may scream and stomp, but they really leave parents out of the equation. Unless, of course, parents insist on climbing into it.

Parents can be on watch for twenty-four hours a day, forever guarding their children against the frustrations, disappointments, and losses that their actions wreak, but at what price, and what messages do such actions

Parents can be on watch for twenty-four hours a day, forever guarding their children against the frustrations, disappointments, and losses that their actions wreak, but at what price?

convey? That the child is so weak and incapable that he'll need eternal coddling from life? Learning how to let natural consequences just be represents a huge boon to one's parenting. It teaches parents that children are much stronger, more robust, and more resilient than we credit them with being. It frees up parenting and takes a lot of responsibility off parents' shoulders, for parents begin to realize that it's OK for kids to know and bear some discomfort. Ultimately, natural consequences enable parents to stay out of the way so that they do not block their child from the very opportunities that will make their child's life better and more doable.

Our actions always have consequences. If life is for learning, and parents' job is to prepare children well for that life, what more relevant, efficient, and compassionate way is there than to allow them to suffer the natural consequences of their actions under parents' loving and watchful eyes?

> Stay empathic with your child's plight, even as you avoid his best efforts to get you to undo the natural consequences of his actions.

As a child my family's menu consisted
of two choices: take it, or leave it.

—Buddy Hackett

16. Refuse to Deal

THE SUSPICION MIGHT BE PLANTED firmly in your head: your child is out to get you. Not like an assassin or anything, though she can sabotage your family in certain ways. Your child has no alternative, perhaps, but to use all of her guile to try to get what she wants. What your child wants, remember, may be nothing like what he psychologically and developmentally needs and may even be something he unconsciously craves. But your child will go for it all the same. He can't help himself; he is a child. We began to address this issue in chapter 11. And by now, maybe you've grown a bit more used to not explaining yourself. But your child's needs and talents for pushing and negotiating will die hard.

Think of a child wheeling and dealing at a cash register: "Please, please, can I get the red ones?" "Please, I promise I will be good all day." "I promise I will help do the dishes." "I promise I won't ask for anything else." "I promise I will give you the extra $20 out of my own money."

No matter how many times you live through this scenario—and no matter how many times your child breaks her promise to help out, behave, not ask for more, or pay you back—if you concede, your child will grow stronger as a negotiator and you will grow weaker. The sad bottom line is that, in doing so, you become a weaker advocate for the parenting and unspoiling that your child needs.

So how can you beat your child at her game? The simple answer is that you can't. When you go head-to-head with your child, you may be playing worse odds than when you play blackjack in Vegas. Your child asks for extra reading at bedtime, and before you know it, she'll be whacking you upside the head with a bait and switch you can't refuse. "Well, if I can't stay up late to have more dessert and play another round of Sorry, then I guess you owe me a back rub and two books before the lights go out." What began as an innocent-looking request for a little extra playtime stealthily turns into the child's last best ultimatum: "Thirty minutes or forty-five minutes more? What's it going to be?"

Say, for example, that you're driving to the grocery store. By the time you park, your child has already asked if he can get some favorite cookies and you've said, "Sure." Nothing wrong with that.

When you go head-to-head with your child, you may be playing worse odds than when you play blackjack in Vegas.

We've all been there. But in the store he soon asks for ice cream and candy, and then wants to critique your shopping up and down twenty-four aisles. What might that sound like?

"Why can't I have candy?"

Because I already...

"But..."

I am not going to say it again.

"Why not?"

I told you once and I…

"You bought Ben…"

I'm buying you cookies. In fact, I let you pick out two kinds of cookies.

"But you got Ben's favorite ice cream, not mine…"

I'm not saying it again. I can't listen to this the whole time I shop…

"But you listen when…"

What's a parent to do? How do you outmaneuver that kind of logic? You refuse to negotiate, as in this example:

"Can I get this ice cream?"

I let you pick out cookies.

"But…"

The mother calmly walks to the cookie aisle, puts the cookies back on the shelf, and heads to the register.

Easy, right?

OK, I admit that I neglected to mention that the boy throws a whopper of a tantrum. He throws stuff out of the cart and makes an unimaginable ruckus at the register. His mother struggles her way out of the store, feeling such humiliation that she swears she'll never shop there again. What could the mother have done when the boy nagged for candy? Better that she'd returned the cookies right then and left sooner. And you're right to ask why she let the boy pick out two kinds of cookies when she'd agreed to only one.

> By learning not to make deals, you spare yourself much parenting energy, time, frustration, and resentment.

Keep in mind that the child does not need a warning each time a parent is about to set a limit. That can backfire and teach a child mostly to be a last-minute reformer. Even as children fight the limits that have been set, most of them understand why parents have done what they have.

What about when the boy commandeered his mother's decision making as to what groceries to buy? She might have tried to shape the boy's arguing into an interesting conversation. But, really, should a child be the head decider and criticize his mother like that?

Should the mother have punished the boy when they got home? No need to. Losing his cookies and leaving the store were the consequences that taught the child his lesson. But the mother can decide not to take the boy to the next thing he wants to go to as a consequence for his rudeness in ruining the shopping trip she needed to go on.

Some might think that the mother could have made both their lives easier and just gone shopping without her son. I could not agree less. These experiences, while trying, are opportunities for both parent and child to learn and build life skills together.

When parents make deals, it is a sign of weakness. They feel as if they cannot close the sale otherwise. But parenting should not be anything like salesmanship. Think of what's involved when you buy a car, and ask yourself whether those are the principles on which you wish to build a relationship with the child you adore, want the best for, and aim to prepare well for life as an adult.

When parents deal, it is a sign of weakness.

I'm not suggesting that children are deviant. I'm

suggesting that by making them avid negotiators, we teach them not to give away anything for free. "If you want a hand bringing in the groceries, then how much is it worth to you?" "I helped rake the leaves, so you owe me $12." "If you want me to do my homework, I think it's only fair that you offer me some sort of compensation or reward." As unbelievable and unreasonable as these sound, it happens all the time—and it works. Parents agree in words or in their actions. Once a child gets paid to hold the door open, he will always want to get paid.

Sometimes the child lives for the negotiating itself. Some children love to deal for the excitement, for the give-and-take with parents. For some children, negotiations are the time when their parents most engage with them, and as we said before, children prefer bad attention to no attention—and negotiating requires a lot of attention.

The solution is to find better ways to give your child attention: "I am done arguing about this. If you'd like to play a game together, I'd love to do so when you're done with your chores. Let me know as soon as you're ready to play." This can work. Just be sure to drop what you are doing as soon as your child has done her duties, met your expectations, and is ready to play.

Parenting without making deals leaves you with straightforward, direct, and clear expectations; limits; consequences; and discipline, too. And lots of love, of course. There is no shortcut to parents earning their children's respect and raising them to be contented, responsible, and grateful adults.

Learn to want your child's unspoiled attitude and behavior as much as she wants to get something or win the struggle. That will help motivate you to do what is needed.

A child, like your stomach, doesn't need
all you can afford to give it.

—FRANK CLARK

17. Buy Less

IMAGINE THIS LIST: "The Top 10 Signs That You May Have Overdone the Kids' Christmas." It might look something like this:

10. Tiffany's asked your daughter to loan back her new necklace for its upcoming global exhibit 150 Years of Diamonds.

9. Your credit card earned enough frequent-flier miles for a round-trip ticket to Tokyo.

8. Laurie Berkner called to ask if you found a guitar tuner in your couch.

7. Your daughter loves her new pet, but it's February and the new stable still doesn't have a roof.

6. Santa billed you for a fuel and weight surcharge.

5. Toys "R" Us changes its name to Toys "R" *You*!

4. The MIT Robotics Lab keeps asking for its cyber-spy prototype back.

3. You're paying to repair the UPS delivery person's double hernia.

2. The tree was gorgeous and the gifts were plenty, but now you have no home to put them in.

And the number one sign that you may have overdone the Holidays [drum roll]:

1. Your children complained and were miserable anyway!

That last line, you know, is often true. Walk around the mall the week after Christmas, and all you hear are children asking their parents for things. I swear there's some basic law of humanity to be had in all this, something like the holiday law: the more stuff a child gets in December, the less stuff the child will remember having gotten by January.

Think of it. Today's stocking stuffers used to be yesterday's main course of presents:

- 1940: "Oh look—a Ping-Pong ball and a Tootsie Roll (the penny size)."
- 1963: "Oh, look—a kitchen-table Ping-Pong set and some Tootsie Rolls (the movie-theater size).
- 2010: "Oh, look—a little blue velvet box in a little blue velvet bag with a shiny sterling-silver bracelet with a silver charm of a Tootsie Roll, and hey, what's with these little squares of chalk?" The parents then explain, all smiles, that the chalk is a clue—to the 760-pound, professional-quality slate pool table with foosball and Ping-Pong attachments that's being delivered next week; that is, if the bay window can be removed for the crane to hoist the table through the dining room. "But don't worry," they assure their children. "That's not your real present. That's just a little something for the whole family."

The more stuff a child gets in December, the less stuff the child will remember having gotten by January.

Downsizing is in. I have seen many articles in parenting magazines that say it is perfectly OK to have a child's party without one of the following: a Lipizzaner pony from the Spanish Riding School in Vienna, a professional clown moonlighting from Ringling Brothers Circus or Cirque du Soleil, a Blue Note recording artist playing jazz versions of Mother Goose, or your state senator or congressional representative reading a proclamation from the governor honoring your child's birthday. In fact, it is even OK not to serve a six-course, catered candlelit dinner.

What happened to make parents feel that a homemade cake and birthday party are not enough? I think the answer is complicated. For some parents, it is just doing more and more, and wanting to do as much as or more than the last party their child went to. Many parents are too busy working to have the energy or motivation to run a homespun party. Some parents feel that what they would make or do would be inadequate. And some children demand that their parties be of such and such a caliber.

But burdened by all of the things that parents heap on them, children are liable to forget things, like how to play by themselves and with others, how to enjoy the outdoors, and so forth. I was very pleased to read that the stick was recently elected to the National Toy Hall of Fame. The committee "praised its all-purpose, all-natural, no-cost qualities" and "noted its ability to serve either as raw material or an appendage transformed by a child's imagination." I suspect that it is only a matter of time before parents run off to stores to buy expensive and mass-produced sticks that are even better than the ones found in nature.

If you're not sure whether you're giving your child too much, check it out. Make a little accounting notebook or create a spreadsheet on your computer. Keep track of every cent you spend on your child for the next seven days. Include everything, not just toys but also admission tickets, the cost of sports equipment and fees, treats, extra desserts, chauffeuring costs, school supplies and clothing, music lessons, and computer stuff. Every time you take out your wallet, and reach for your credit card or checkbook, ask yourself whether the expense is for your child. If it is, tally it up. Add all the costs up as a whole and by categories. See what you think. I bet it is much more than you ever realized.

> Be careful that family vacations don't also mean vacations from reasonable and budget-wise spending. Few things sting as badly as credit card charges for vacation extravagances that linger from that family trip you took months ago.

So what are the secrets to spending less money on your child? First, open your wallet or pocketbook less often, and when you do, take less money from it. Second, forbid your children from opening your wallet or pocketbook and taking money from it. Third, use your credit cards less—they are basically the same as taking money from your wallet, only you have to pay it back at the end of the month, unless, of course, you go bankrupt and you don't have to. Hurray!

This may sound too simplistic and like old news. But that, to a large extent, is where a major piece of the problem resides. If you were able to spend less on your child, your child would, at least materially speaking, be less spoiled—much less. And the simple act of spending less would bring with it many other substantial benefits of unspoiling. For example, you would spend less time driving around or browsing the Internet to spend money. You and your child would have more time to do things other than buying and returning. Maybe treks to the woods or bike rides to the park could replace some of your trips to the mall. Spending less and not straining your budget might make you less stressed—and on and on. Although spending less is not the silver bullet of unspoiling, it is a major weapon in your arsenal.

Of course, your child's will to resist your new frugality might be formidable. And you can't simply blame her for that. According to Susan Linn's book *Consuming Kids*, each year children spend more than $18 billion, influence purchases totaling more than $600 billion, and watch about 40 thousand commercials. What's more, 65 percent of children eight years old and older have televisions in their own rooms. Linn, an expert on the effects of advertising on children, says that even babies request brand names soon after they learn to speak. That's just some of what children are up against, which means that's what their parents are up against too.

And don't bother asking your young child if he thinks money grows on trees. Your two-year-old will only laugh at you, for even he knows that the answer is no. Money

Giving children too much, today and tomorrow, can deprive them of more precious and profound gifts, such as patience, contentment, consideration, and other skills that help make for a rich, successful, and fulfilled existence.

doesn't grow on trees; it's made in ATM machines.

The following paragraphs discuss some things to think about when you go shopping, especially around the holidays.

Hold on to your budget. Figure out what you can afford to spend on gifts. Be realistic and fair to your financial situation. The first principle of any gift giving is that it should do you no financial harm.

Be conservative. Some years are bountiful, and some are leaner. Try not to spend money you won't receive until the future. By the time tomorrow comes, you will surely have new bills and new necessities. Spend as if your economic future will be more like your average week of income, not your best week.

Remember your priorities. Remind yourself of the other things you need money for, things such as braces for the children's teeth, night school (to improve your life and career), a bathroom remodeling, or maybe just to maintain a small emergency fund for the family and home. Beware that the pressure to buy holiday gifts doesn't set your more important plans backward or utterly derail your saving for things that matter more in your and your family's life.

Hang tough. When the enthusiasm and fatigue of holiday shopping get to you, it is all too easy to buy a little or a lot more. Stay mentally tough and keep asking yourself, "Does my child really need this? Will she really use it? Is it really worth all that money? Have I already bought enough?" Talk to yourself as if you are a trusted financial adviser or a critical parent who thinks you overindulge your child.

Think quality, not quantity. How many gifts does a child need to feel loved or remembered on the holidays? Probably fewer than she gets. For example, stocking stuffers used to mean little curiosities and candies to decorate the mantel the night before Christmas. Resist that nagging doubt to keep buying one more thing.

Look in the parenting mirror. Children who are given too much on the holidays are often the same children who are spoiled the rest of the year. There's no better time to readjust your parenting and get some good unspoiling going than during the holidays. No child ever suffered from having a reasonable season of gifts.

Plan and keep to your plan. Nothing brings out the most unwise, unnecessary, and wasteful spending than last-minute holiday shopping. Strive not to leave shopping for the last week, especially if you have a tendency toward the holiday crazies. Though most parents don't like to admit it, many fear that they haven't gotten enough for the children, as if there have to be a certain number of boxes to guarantee a joyous celebration. In such moments, parents are vulnerable to buying impulsively and needlessly. Such last-minute cramming can wholly ruin a kept-to holiday budget or can push an overblown budget and debt farther out of control.

Keep the spirit away from your wallet. Watch that nostalgia for the holidays of your childhood doesn't open your pocketbook as much as your heart. The holidays for many people have come to have limited religious meaning, because corporate forces have single-handedly turned them into industries. Parents' gift giving can, I fear, further undermine whatever deeper meanings the holidays can carry.

Think character. A majority of parents, both married and single, live on a budget. But for those who are lucky to have more, recall that just because you can afford it doesn't mean it's good for your children. Children who are spoiled on the holidays often are children who are spoiled every other day of the year. Giving children too much, today and tomorrow, can deprive them of more precious and profound gifts, such as patience, contentment, consideration, and other skills that help make for a rich, successful, and fulfilled existence.

A child can be spoiled with purchases that can appear to be necessities, such as school supplies, clothing, books, sports equipment, and the like. Many guitar greats, including B. B. King, Eric Clapton, and Pat Metheny, started out with cheap instruments. Why does your beginning musician or athlete need professional-quality equipment?

Where parents do too much for their children,
the children will not do much for themselves.

—ELBERT HUBBARD

18. Develop Real Winners

WE'VE BEEN TURNING our children into blue-ribbon losers. Don't believe me? Look at the statistics on teen anxiety, depression, alcohol and drug use, cheating, suicide, self-injury, and so on.

The eminently wise education writer Alfie Kohn makes the case convincingly. Young children work to please their parents. They strive to do things that will elicit their parents' approving smiles and warm glow of pride. These children will work for stickers and gold stars that say, "Job well done." Over time, these external rewards become part of the children's internal motivation, so that they want to do well to please themselves. As a result, they will naturally come to value their own learning and achievements.

Gaining the approval of others is part of children's growth. We never stop needing some of that. But we have to find a way to get over our compulsive need to celebrate—meaning reward, note, confirm, or spotlight—every step the child takes, whether big or little, accomplished or failed, new or old, well earned or earned by happenstance. We are creating a generation of children who cannot live without the constant spotlight, without someone on the outside forever stamping what they do as worthwhile and grand.

At what age do children start to roll their eyes when they get trophies for sports they dislike and for which they've never produced a drop of sweat? Go to any recital and look at all the accolades for children studying piano or violin. There's an entire cottage industry built around our obsession, and thick catalogs featuring an

> *We are creating a generation of children who cannot live without the constant spotlight.*

infinite assortment of "prizes": Beethoven plastic key rings, Mozart cups, Chopin retractable pens.

But the bone I'm picking is not with coaches or music teachers. At least they can point to a body of work that deserves note—the child came to a season of soccer or practiced piano daily for a year. Contrast that with the body of work that parents are prone to honor:

- "Wow, you did a great job brushing your teeth."
- "Wow, you did a great job eating lunch."
- "Wow, you're having so much fun playing with that new toy."
- "Wow, what a great job you did sleeping."
- "Wow, you did a great job picking up those blocks. And Daddy only asked eleven times!"
- "Wow, you did a great job inhaling oxygen and exhaling carbon dioxide. We are so proud of you!"

> Accomplishment and being able to put out a good effort can be rewards in themselves.

OK, I made my point. But this is a big problem and one that can potentially harm your child. It is also a problem that you can handily discharge and remedy. How?

Foremost, change your mind-set. Does anyone notice and praise your every step and breath? Why, barely anyone notices that you hobble through the house with a broken foot. Life is tough. A child who's addicted to perpetual celebration will suffer much in a world that will often be busy with other things and people.

Does this mean you should ignore your child? Not at all. It means you should reserve praise for worthy achievement, most of all for achievement that requires effort. Your child does not need to get a prize for being able to decide between two toys in less than half an hour or for not biting the cat.

This is a huge distinction, a crucial one that, if missed, can cause parents to dismiss this whole unspoiling routine. "But he says we can't praise our child!" That's not what I'm saying. What I'm saying is this: reward the effort, the attempt, and the trying, and not the mundane, the routine, and the obvious.

Your child does deserve notice and validation for trying hard to be and do better. "Wow, your little sister just grabbed your new toy, and you didn't even hit her." "Wow, you tried to put your dish in the dishwasher just like we do." "Wow, you shut off that video game even though you wanted to keep playing; that must have been hard." Don't save flattery only for when your child is being good. Give acclaim for effort and attempts to do better. "I can see you're trying very hard not to lose your temper." If anything, this is what your child wants you to validate.

With respect to children's grades, some parents offer $50 for each A, $30 for each B, and $15 for each C, and a $75 bonus for making the honor roll. Other parents disagree with the whole idea of paying your child cash for grades. They prefer a small token of acknowledgment, a symbolic gesture, something like the U2 commemorative iPod or a vintage Stratocaster.

Reward the effort, the attempt, and the trying, not the mundane, the routine, and the obvious.

You know my feelings on bribing your children for good work. How about a different kind of gift? Statements like: "Wow, it must feel good to see all your hard work pay off." "Your teachers noticed all that you did." "You must be so proud!" To be able to say such things, you have to take your child's perspective, remember all of her studying, and leave yourself out of the equation, allowing the report card and all that it represents to be his alone.

Sometimes a parent's smile, knowing glance, pat on the shoulder, or simple statement—"You should be so proud of what you've done"—is both sufficient and special. Doling these out hourly, undeservedly, or insincerely will soon ruin their charm and powers, however.

If you want children to keep their feet on the ground, put some responsibility on their shoulders.

—ABIGAIL VAN BUREN

19. Work Them

MUCH OF THE SELF-ESTEEM MOVEMENT, as we've already discussed, has proved disastrous. Parents were mistakenly advised that if they bathed their children in love and admiration, they would thrive as adults who, deep inside, felt thoroughly wonderful and worthy. But this approach didn't create contented, productive, glowing individuals. Just the opposite. We now know that constant stroking doesn't build good self-esteem as much as it barely maintains self-esteem that's shaky and in need of constant buttressing. We've talked about the best ways to provide praise and admiration. But what are the best ways to build self-esteem?

It's actually a strong sense of competency that endows a child with hardy self-esteem. So how does a parent foster a child's sense of competency? By creating opportunities for that child to face and master challenges. These challenges do not have to be enormous. We are not talking Mount Everest or memorizing the dictionary. I refer to the challenges that make up what most of us take to be everyday life.

> *A strong sense of competency endows a child with hardy self-esteem.*

Learning to walk, to put on one's own socks, to use the toilet, and to sleep in a crib are early aspects of that natural drive to do for oneself. Remember "Mommy, I brushed my own teeth"? Many parents look at their now seemingly helpless teenagers and wonder where all that prideful independence vanished.

Let your child assert her independence and follow her lead. If she asks for help putting a red piece on her Lego creation, refrain from adding green, blue, and black. Want to see indignation in the raw? Help a young child more than he wants to be helped. Grrrrrrr!

When a growing child asks for help, it is usually because he is stuck and frustrated and wants just enough assistance so that he can speedily get back to his adventure of self-actualization. So, one way that we foster a sense of competence is by staying out of the way and trying not to block the child's innate drive toward mastery and autonomy.

We guide children, for example, by making sure that they don't hurt themselves with knives or kitchen gadgetry when attempting to make us breakfast. Yet we don't squash or in any way demoralize their forward march and earnest ambition. Want to see utter frustration and disappointment? When your child clumsily tries to clean up a dirt mess with the new broom, scream, "You're only making more of a mess!" *But don't you see*, your child wants to say, *I'm trying to clean it. Show me how, so that I can clean it up myself!*

When I was growing up, my own father didn't see this. Even when I was a teen, he'd expect me to hold the screwdriver or even just the screw for fifteen minutes while he did the work. I was a human tool belt, and I would often grow bored just standing there and would end up juggling, dropping, and misplacing the screw. What might he have done? Let me do the screwdriving and hammering while he assisted and guided me. Those parents I see who have their toddlers using child-sized garden tools know what they're doing, empowering their little children to rake (and contribute, and work) alongside them. Children don't just want to play kitchen, they want to be cooking in the real kitchen.

> Being engaged with a parent—working alongside a parent, for instance—can be a child's greatest reward and motivator.

At the peril of giving away my age and sounding like a grumpy old man, I offer my observation that upcoming generations seem to lack a work ethic. Several years ago, I worked with a wayward but recovering teen who wanted to work with cars. A local garage owner generously offered him a job. The teen lasted two days. "I'm not gonna spend my life sweeping floors and doing oil changes," the boy complained (with some choicer words thrown in). That the successful garage owner still himself swept the floor and did oil changes didn't matter. This teenager wanted to be working on fine European automobiles; scratch that, he deserved to be working on such automobiles.

Just as it takes waiting to learn patience and not getting to learn gratitude, learning to work comes about only by actually working. There just isn't any other way.

Well before your child has the physical strength, ability, and sense to help in any significant way, you can start to foster a work ethic. Of course, I realize that the ways a young child can work are limited and that tasks have to be scaled accordingly. Though, for example, even at a young age my son could truly help us reorganize kitchen cabinets and closets, and my daughter could do serious gardening and snow shoveling when working by our sides and under our guidance. Capitalize on your young child's eagerness to be your little helper. Invite your toddler to help you around the house. Let her hold onto the vacuum or hammer beside your hand. As your toddler grows, show him what he can do and give him reasonable tasks. Make helping you an enjoyable and satisfying time, not one of criticism and perfectionism.

Encouraging and allowing a young child to work is a lot of work for the parent. You can probably vacuum much more quickly by yourself than while vacuuming alongside a kindergartner, however hard he might try. And you could wax and polish your car, perhaps, in less time than it will take your child to change into car-washing clothes. But what is your mission—productivity or teaching your child?

Children who learn to like working at a young age tend to carry that good feeling and personal commitment in them throughout their adolescence and lifetime. They will, on their own, seek out more responsibility as their maturing bodies and minds enable them to. Be careful that your affluence does not dissuade you from creating conditions for your child to want to work, for that would deprive your child of valuable education.

The lessons we seek to teach children about work are multifaceted. We want to teach them a basic work ethic, a capacity and a willingness to work hard. By teaching them to help us work at a level that they can relate to, we start to teach them real work skills, such as how to garden, how to do housework and carpentry, and so on. When you engage them in work that relates directly to your existence—such as cooking food that you eat or building something that you use—you give them a real connection to their world and their place in it. We, as a society, are far removed from the earth and from sources of sustenance. Doing basic labor is healthy, restorative, and psychologically fulfilling for both adults and children. By involving children, for example, in designing and buying materials to build a birdhouse, you can start to teach planning, organizational, and creative skills. And whatever kind of work you bring the child into, you give a loud and clear message that work is a good and valuable way to spend time. Work is, after all, one way in which people find lifelong purpose and meaning.

By teaching children to help us work at a level that they can relate to, we start to teach them real work skills.

Should you pay your child for work he does? This is a bit different from the kind of bribing I was talking about earlier. Here I'm talking about an allowance for chores, a highly debated issue with no one right answer. Some people believe in allowances that require work, such as family chores. Some parents don't like that and believe that children should freely contribute to the household work as part of their being in a family. I have no problem with either, as long as you get the child working. I am not suggesting that you pay your child for reasonable age-related tasks, like brushing teeth, doing homework, or cleaning her own room. That would be unconstructive bribery. Here, I refer to extra chores or work that you judge to be within the child's abilities.

As I've mentioned, I do see trouble brewing when even young children have to be paid to do anything helpful. Some parents go so far as to pay their children adult-sized salaries for child-sized workloads. That is unnecessary and unwise. It is fine, I think, to pay children a fair wage for fair work that goes beyond weekly kinds of chores.

But think twice before paying for work that is undone or poorly done. Rather than withholding pay, a better solution is to ask your child to remedy the work performance (according to their ability, of course).

Creative writing professors don't praise end product as much as they praise the process of learning. Think of "teaching" your children about work and life in the same way.

The other night I ate at a real nice family restaurant. Every table had an argument going.

—GEORGE CARLIN

20. Unspoil in Public

WE ALL KNOW THE SCENE, and most of us have lived it ourselves. You say no, and the children say yes. You say no again; they say yes again. It starts to get louder and more disorganized, and you feel that you are rapidly becoming a spectacle of human tragedy: parenting at its worst. At these inevitable and awful moments, your choices seem to dwindle, and you soon forget your bigger vision and goals for unspoiling.

You can push your unspoiling agenda, but at what risk? You can set your limits and stand firm, then step aside to let your child blow like Mount St. Helens. Who cares about the noise or that your child's writhing body lays across an aisle, blocking dozens of shoppers and their carts? Who cares that you're getting the evil eye from everyone? Who cares? You do.

And what's the alternative? If you've ever watched an episode of tough-love-no-matter-what at your local mall, you know it is a hard one to watch. Children scream bloody murder as their heartless parents walk on. Children hang on to their parents' feet, kicking and yelling and saying heartwarming things such as "I hate you" and "You're the worst parent in the world."

Parenting in public can be as tough as it gets. Few people willingly sign up for reality television; most of us prefer that our ugliest and most hapless parenting stays out of view. My experience tells me that a lot of parents deal with such dilemmas by using a two-point strategy. First, they try to prevent such moments from happening, not by mastering the circumstances but by avoiding the situation altogether. They go shopping without their children, for example. Second, they sidestep and finesse their way around it, which means they basically try to give in just enough to stop the fuss; get the kid off the floor and out of the store; and move the whole shenanigans back home, where at least they don't have to be publicly humiliated. For some families, this is a once-in-a-while happening. For others, it is life as usual.

Parenting in public can be as tough as it gets.

Avoidance, such as never taking the kids to a store, is a poor solution. How will your children learn to handle life, and how will you learn to handle your children? Moreover, if you never pursue your unspoiling in public, you will compromise your effort, sort of like handcuffing one unspoiling hand behind your back, especially the hand that you use to take away things.

One mother posed it to me in this way. "It's kind of weird. My children's spoiled behavior totally embarrasses me in public, and yet I can take that more easily than I can trying to set limits and just failing in front of everyone." Feeling ineffective as a parent is awful. Feeling ineffective under the critical eyes of the world at large is awful to the tenth power. But you must learn to unspoil in public if you are going to unspoil your child at all.

You must learn to unspoil in public if you are going to unspoil your child at all.

If you find it near impossible to unspoil your child in public, start curtailing your excursions out into the world. Start small, and work your way back out. It won't take very long. Let your child know that you and he won't be going to stores or the mall until behaviors get better. But let him know that you are hopeful that things will turn around soon, and that you will give him lots of chances and help behaving well outside of the house. If staying in is a big problem for you, you might enlist someone's help to watch the child until you can solve the problem.

Next plan a short and sweet public outing. Run one simple errand perhaps, such as going to the dry cleaner rather than getting a week's worth of groceries at the chaotic supermarket. Let your child know what you will be doing, not in a threatening way, but in terms of information. "OK, we're going to pick up some clothes from the dry cleaner." Prepare your child briefly. "You might be bored. Do you want to bring a book or something?" Leave it up to your child to decide and get what she wants to take. (Beware of training your child to see and use you as her personal pack mule.)

> If your child routinely disrupts other children's parties, consider banning him from parties until he shows true motivation to behave there.

When you get to the dry cleaner, look at your child and, in a kindly but clear voice, let her know your expectations of her in the dry cleaner. Pay attention to your child while waiting in the dry cleaner. Engage him. "Is it hard waiting?" "Look at that sign, what do you think it is?" As you are leaving the store, let him know that you noticed his effort. "You really worked to be patient in there, didn't you?" Remember, notice the process and effort more than you praise or reward the outcome. Once you are back home, acknowledge your child's effort again. "Thanks for being so patient [or helpful] at the dry cleaner."

A few points to remember. First, go slowly and build on each success. Do not graduate from a fifteen-minute trip to the dry cleaner to a whole-day multistate shopping spree. Second, go frequently. Instead of hours of errands, break them up into several trips. Going and returning home and getting in and out of the car is part of the solution. Getting your child comfortable with and able to handle transitions is a good life skill. Third, do not bribe. Fourth, be patient and thoughtful. Your sole goal is to promote the next success. Five, and most important, engage your child in a relationship while you're out in public. Some children unreasonably want all of the attention all of the time. However, in this new day of technology, I've witnessed children dragged along by parents who never get off the cell phone and seldom address the child except to reprimand them. Talk to your child and interact while you're out in public.

If your child is fine while you run his errands but then refuses to run yours, it's time to regrab his attention (revisit chapter 5).

> If, when you're outside your home, you find other adults unexpectedly helping keep your children safe or in line without prompting from you, take the hint.

Unspoiling in front of family, such as grandparents, can feel tantamount to unspoiling in public. Some grandparents critique the spoiling of their grandchildren. This can be painful and a source of great friction. Look in the mirror and admit all that is true about your parenting and your child. Ask yourself this: when it comes to the grandparents, am I mostly killing the messengers of a reality that I'd rather not see? Once you've clarified that, work to improve communications with the grandparents. Ask to have a discussion. Tell them that you share their concern but that it is hurtful to have them roll their eyes or make comments about your child or your parenting. Offer ways that they can share and support your unspoiling effort.

Other grandparents spoil grandchildren excessively, much to the parents' chagrin. Such grandparents indulge out of love, of course. If you feel that your parents or in-laws are making it worse or are affecting your child adversely, gently talk with them about your own struggles with indulging. Ask them, perhaps, for their support and help in unspoiling your child. Let them know that you value the love and attention that they give your child, but that, at least for now, you are trying to unspoil. If you feel comfortable doing so, open a channel of communication that invites your parents' input and observations. Maybe share this book with them, and cultivate a dialogue together. (Even as I write this, I think of parents who only wish that their children had overly involved and giving grandparents.) Once your unspoiling regimen is solidly established and working, grandparents' indulging will be secondary and relatively irrelevant. However, even then, you can help teach grandparents other ways of showing love, whether by giving attention, playing games, buying fewer and less expensive gifts, and so forth.

To bring up a child in the way he should go,
travel that way yourself once in a while.

—JOSH BILLINGS

21. Unspoil Yourself

LAST YEAR WHILE WAITING for my order at a well-known dark-roasted-coffee shop, I watched a father who was out with his three young children for a late-afternoon snack. It was hard not to notice as he coaxed and cajoled his children to hurry up and make a decision as to what they wanted. After a lot of hemming and hawing, the children unanimously decided on hot chocolates, large. But the father ordered his children three small drinks and limited them to one dessert each. When the register rang somewhere at more than $25, the father looked at me and rolled his eyes.

"What am I supposed to do?" he asked rhetorically. "Just get myself a coffee and tell them they can't have anything?"

I smiled and nodded—no kidding, I've been there, done that.

My example might be a bad one, for my message is not about what the children got, well, not exactly, though we'll soon see that's it's all related. I mean to call attention to the father and his coffee. Many parents today are equally tempted to indulge themselves as their children. They wait in lines for expensive coffees and drink bottled waters, and that's just the little stuff. They buy cars with accessories and luxury to match their living rooms, no matter the cost or fuel economy. They have fantasies of, if not plans for, bigger, better, and remodeled homes, not to mention five-star vacations and everything else. On and on—you're as qualified as I am to fill in the blanks.

Many parents today are equally tempted to indulge themselves as their children.

The same children who drive their parents crazy with their unreasonable and unrelenting

170

demands watch their parents pursue their own versions of instant gratification. The second the parent has a need or want, they jump in the car and drive to the mall, and the kids tag along. Or faster yet, parents jump onto their computers, computers that can never go fast enough, and buy items that'll be delivered the next morning. Is there any doubt that people would pay for next-hour delivery if FedEx offered it?

The same children who drive their parents crazy with their demands for that blue bowl or that one cereal watch their parents drive miles upon local miles to get themselves this wine, that beer, or a must-see movie. The same children who drive their parents crazy with screams that they're starving or dying of thirst watch their parents stop, even on the shortest of errand runs, to hop in or drive through for a nonfat latte with two peppermint pumps. The same children who drive their parents crazy with unending requests for stuff watch and hear their parents always talking about the stuff they want and dream of. And those same children who drive their parents crazy with all of that behavior watch their parents display exactly that same behavior.

Many parents do not fit this mode at all. And

further, I know that doing so is hardly parents' fault. I also know how I like my coffee and my music. Parents have understandably fallen victim to a world that is just too seductive, too full of choice, too abundant. Corporate greed, and its disciple, modern advertising, pound at us like a northeast wind that never lets up. I'm just pointing out that our grown-up experience and susceptibility should caution us as to what our children confront.

What can parents do? Move to an island? Impractical. Set their time machines back? From what I've been reading, they will have to go way back. Even Wilma Flintstone longed for the latest fashions, and Fred for the newest automobile. I'm afraid we are fixed where we are, left to plod along as best we can. And so we'll do our best to regularly look in the parenting mirror and reassess our home life. Just as it's never too late to grow less indulgent with the children, it is never too late to do so with ourselves, as parents. It is never too late to start watching the examples that we set and change them when warranted.

I am not suggesting that you deny yourself or wage a single-handed, self-sacrificing war against corporate

America. (Though any efforts you make to resist or counter its pressures are admirable and worthwhile.) I am only suggesting that parents keep their own behaviors in mind.

Although there are hundreds of quotable statements about parents and children, Albert Schweitzer said it

It is never too late to start watching the examples that we set.

well. "Adults teach children in three important ways: The first is by example, the second is by example, the third is by example." Young children adore their parents and look to them for the answers to all things and all of life. Many believe that the examples we set influence our children even more than our parenting words or deeds, our purposeful efforts to raise children well.

And, I suppose, it's probably not getting fancy coffees to go that mostly affects our children, but our drive to consume, to spend inordinate amounts of our day shopping or planning for shopping. Some children hear this throughout the day: "I've got to get over to such and such for the sale." "Remind me, we need to buy…" And "I'll pick that up at the mall this afternoon." Shopping is a full-time avocation for some people. What else do some children hear? They hear parents complain about what they have, don't have, or wish they could have. How can this example not trickle (or avalanche) down on the children and have an impact on them?

Keeping up with the neighbors is one of the major pressures that parents can face. When we put effort into and spend money to keep up an image, we implicitly make a decision to forsake other values and ways of living. It can take a certain courage to guide your life differently, and it can be freeing, too, if that is the path you wish for you, your children, and your parenting.

I am not recommending that you shred your credit cards and grow all the food you need at home. There are matters of degrees. Parents can tone down their consumerism and help guard their children against the rampant materialism in society. Downsizing does not have to be an either/or proposition. Observe yourself for a day or two, watch what you shop and buy for, listen to what you talk about, ponder what keeps popping into mind, and what the compass for your day and living looks like. You'll know best what to make of it and what to do, if anything.

> Coming to better understand your own discontent will benefit your children and your unspoiling, but it can make you happier, too.

If you wish to downsize your spending and consumerism, not just for your children's sake or for the sake of unspoiling, then there are many ways to begin—and opportunities to include your child as well. You can do it kind of quietly, living it yourself and letting the children follow. Or you can do it more consciously, by having a discussion with your child about your beliefs and how you are going to change some of the ways you have been living—in age-appropriate terms, of course. Hearing that water is polluted, the sun is burning out, and the ozone is disappearing may frighten a young child. (If you need ideas about how to talk about such things, take a peek at some science and nature magazines for children.)

Many consumers describe their shopping as almost an addiction. This suggests that stopping or cutting back can be hard but worthwhile. You will have to work at it. Downsizing may not fix things quickly.

Go through all of your stuff—the kind of stuff that we need bigger basements and attics to hold. Sort through it, with your child's help, perhaps. Give away what others can use. Recycle other things. Find new uses for old things. Explain, too, how your new beliefs are going to change the way you shop and buy stuff. Offer your child exciting, adventurous, and healthy alternatives to shopping, things that young kids love, such as gardening, making things, cooking, and so forth, activities that invite creativity and personal investment.

Too often we give children answers to remember
rather than problems to solve.

—ROGER LEWIN

22. Promote Self-Sufficiency

PARENTS WHO STRUGGLE with their indulged children are often taken aback when teachers report that those same children are model citizens at school. When they visit the school, parents cannot believe their eyes when they see toddlers picking up toys, rolling up mats, and maintaining cubbies and personal stuff all by themselves.

"He'd never ever do that at home. He'd never do that for me," parents say to the teachers. "He has no choice here. We expect it," the teachers reply. "Expect it"—now there's an idea.

Children are born with a love of learning and a love of doing things by themselves. We, as parents, have become very good at doing everything to squash and extinguish that impetus toward autonomy.

We should nurture "I can do it myself," that healthy credo by which toddlers live, as if it's the last living plant on earth. Instead, we run around watering the rocks and the sand. What goes wrong? How is it that we celebrate our children's strivings for independence but later push them to regress?

Maybe we don't fully understand what it means. I suppose it is cute and adorable when a toddler washes her own hands or dresses herself or sits at the dinner table properly. But those actions mean a lot more than that. They are the beginning of a long process by which a child grows more capable and trusting of her powers and abilities.

Children are born with a love of learning and a love of doing things by themselves.

Believing in herself and assuming responsibility contribute to the child's growing confidence and resilience. How can that be anything but good?

I have a particularly vivid memory of my grown daughter as a child. It was early morning, before the sun had come up. I'd gotten out of bed to go check on the rustling I heard coming from the kitchen.

As I walked down the stairs, I saw that the kitchen light was on. It was clear to me that my two-year-old daughter was up to something. I peeked through the doorway, and there Hannah was in her powder-blue pajamas. She had dragged a large wooden chair over to the kitchen counter and had already climbed on top. I quietly watched with amazement as she hauled herself up the cabinet shelves to reach the very top, where she stretched her fingers to haul in a can of her favorite snack food.

"Whatcha doing?" I so startled poor Hannah that she almost fell off the chair she was coming down.

Wow, just two years old and capable of going out into the dark house by herself and down the hallway to the kitchen, where she single-handedly moved heavy furniture to climb to a midnight snack. Just ponder the initiative, the athleticism, the ingenuity, and the problem solving—not to mention the love of carbo-hydrates—that went into her adventure. And she did it all by herself. Of course, if this had blossomed into a regular and dangerous progression of behavior, I'd have had to curb it. But it didn't.

Now contrast that scenario with one of the typical teenager in the typical home: A teen lays on the couch, wrapped in a blanket, having just gotten up sometime on a Saturday afternoon. His mother, who has been up since dawn and has already done a weekend's work, puts away groceries that she shopped for and carried in by herself.

"Will you give me the remote?" the fit and strong fifteen-year-old asks his mother as he feebly stretches his arm out from under the blanket to point at the remote that lays on the coffee table a foot or so out of his reach. His mother puts the bag she's carrying down and walks across the kitchen to hand him the remote.

"I don't get why you need me to get you the remote. You're right next to it, and I'm busy putting away the groceries."

"It's cooold."

The mother goes back to the groceries.

"Will you pour me a glass of milk?"

The mother gives her son an I-can't-believe-how-lazy-you-are look as she walks to the fridge and pours her son a glass of milk, which she then delivers to him on the couch.

"And a sandwich, too?" he peeps from under the blanket. "Please?" spoken like a four-year-old.

This scenario takes place in family rooms everywhere and forever repeats itself. "I don't get why you need me to get you a glass of milk. You're right next to it, and I'm busy putting away the groceries." Indeed, none of us get it. And yet we still fetch him the remote.

Let's apply a little logic, the kind that most every parent possesses and can readily use when it comes to other people's children and homes. If children at the age of two are capable of so much, why do they need a grown-up to wait on them at ages five or nine or sixteen? Doing too much for your child, not making him wait a second, and being at her beck and call are all variations on spoiling. I

If children at the age of two are capable of so much, why do they need a grown-up to wait on them at ages five or nine or sixteen?

know parents are busy, and enforcing this kind of self-reliance might be more than you can manage.

But it is worthwhile to create the conditions under which your child can learn to do more and more on her own safely and with some success. As a simple example, if a child wants to wash her own hands, a sturdy and child-safe step stool might enable her to keep her hands and face clean. A child's wish to feed himself should likewise be supported. If he makes a mess that is insufferable, figure out some way he can feed himself without too much cleanup for you. As children grow older, they may wish to do other things by themselves (though that probably won't include cleaning up after themselves). Spend some time figuring out ways that you can help your child do it on her own in a way that you can live with. It takes time, effort, and patience for parents to allow children to exercise their drive toward self-sufficiency, yet it's a worthwhile endeavor.

In your efforts to prevent or undo spoiling, if your child says he can't do something when you know he can, follow your own good sense. If your child is in need of more attention or caring, give it to him. However, if you feel that your child is indulged or gets plenty of TLC, you can hang back and make your expectations clear as to what he can do.

For example, if your child is screaming for you to go get her boots in her closet and put them on her feet, you can say something like, "We'll go to the park as soon as you get your boots from your room and put them on. I'll wait here, and we'll go as soon as you're ready." When you start to feel irritated or resentful over things that you are doing for your child, whatever your child's age, it might be a sign that you are doing too much.

When your child acts babyish, rather than show exasperation or denigrate those actions, kindly summon more grown-up behavior. "I'll get the plate and knife. You get the peanut butter. And then you can make us both lunch!"

Parents must balance being supportive and protective with empowering the child to be his own advocate, especially around teachers and other adults. Parents accomplish this by watching closely, listening, and by trial and error. Young children obviously need more help, especially with big things. But I've seen even first and second graders learn to advocate for themselves with teachers and such. This, too, is part of unspoiling: it means that the child is expected to assume some responsibility for her own destiny as it makes itself known in her daily life, a much bigger and deeper version of getting your own glass of milk. Children who learn to watch out for and assert themselves are well prepared for life.

Children tend to appreciate and feel respected when their parents ask them directly, "Would you like me to call your teacher, or would you rather tell her yourself?" There is almost no age at which this simple question isn't relevant and useful. Parents who are forever complaining to the school and teachers on their child's behalf should stop and think about what their actions might be telling their child. For children, learning to get along with teachers is an important life lesson that will serve them well throughout their education and future work life.

Many years ago, we hired a high school sophomore to baby-sit for our children. She asked for something like $9 an hour, which was kind of high even then. A month later, her mother wrote us a scathing letter saying that we should have paid her $13 like the other girls in their neighborhood got. In my opinion, this mother did her daughter a disservice. "It's your job," many of our own parents would have said to us at that age. "Work it out on your own."

Of course, parents can help their children in many ways to grow to be strong and self-sufficient. We can think aloud to model good problem solving. We can show them how to put our feelings in place and how we manage our anger so those feelings do not undermine our efforts. We can help children plan what they wish to say or let them rehearse with us, and so on. In short, we can do everything to help empower their self-sufficiency in managing the bumps in their lives. And we can let them know that if they want it or need it, we can always step in to help them.

Letting children try to solve their own problems, when practical, lends them resilience that will buttress them for a lifetime.

*Children begin by loving their parents; as they grow
older they judge them; sometimes they forgive them.*

—OSCAR WILDE

23. Make Room for Amends

I BET YOU'VE HEARD or said all of the following:

- "I'm sorry."
- "Really, I am sorry."
- "I am very sorry."
- "Sorrrrryyyyy," said with an adorable, mopey puppy face.
- "Say you're sorry."
- "Go tell Aunt Sally that you're sorry."
- "I'm sorry I hurt your feelings, Aunt Sally," in sing-song, an inaudible mumble, or at seventy-five miles per hour.

Getting your child to say sorry can be easy or daunting. Some children stubbornly resist saying it. I have no strong opinion on whether it is a worthwhile battle for a parent to fight. Children can learn to say the emptiest of sorries. Think of boys who fight on the playground. Sworn enemies, they do as the principal mandates. "Sorry." "Sorry." Handshake. "Quite right and cheerio," and everybody's happy.

I have no problem with peacemaking and its etiquette, but that begs the more important task of helping children cope with feelings of being sorry and taking the proper action of remedy. We care about this because children can be spoiled in the sense of not having to bear and live by the norms that guide the rest of us in our interactions. Children can be spoiled if they believe they need to neither regret their actions nor exert any real effort to make amends. At the extreme, children can find other people's hurt feelings irritating and angering.

> *Children can be spoiled if they believe they need to neither regret their actions nor exert any real effort to make amends.*

One of the best ways to promote your child's capacity for being sorry is to watch for, listen to, and stroke his heartfelt remorse when he is young. For instance, if a toddler spills a glass of milk and rushes clumsily to clean it up, let him do it. Yes, you can shape his behavior, helping him to learn how to clean up a little better. But, after all, he is only a toddler.

In contrast, consider these three examples. First, the parent says, "Get out of here, you've already made enough mess." The child hears, *I did something really bad, and I am really bad. I can't pour milk and I can't clean up.* Second, the parent says: "No, no, I'll clean up. You're only making it worse." The child hears everything the first child heard, only more so. Third, the parent says, "From now, I'll pour the milk around here." The child hears, *I can't pour milk. I can't clean up. I can't grow up to do things for myself.* And the most dangerous of all, *I can't undo my mistakes.*

What might parents do instead? Let children clean up their mess—and make their amends—as best as their abilities allow. Offer gently to help a child clean, assisting her rather than making her assist you. Acknowledge her wish to make it right, and show your appreciation for her doing so. "You wanted to clean it up. Thank you!" This is not the moment to teach your child how to pour milk or clean spills. Those are trivial lessons. It is the time to teach your child how to feel remorse and fix it. And you did that just by affirming his own healthy inclination to clean up his mess and make it OK. Isn't that a life skill that will well serve every child and adult!

By far, the most natural and constructive way a child can convey being sorry is by feeling a desire to somehow make up for it. Parents seldom allow their young children to make amends. They prefer, so it seems, to spotlight children's errors so the children simply say a heartfelt apology. But children often feel a deeper need to make up for their errors, to restore others' view of them and their own good view of themselves.

When children can undo what they did, it clears the slate and makes them not feel so bad and endows them with a miraculously resilient power. Mistakes, they learn, can be corrected. They also learn the more profound truth that relationships, too, can be fixed.

When your son breaks your favorite glass and offers to buy you a new one, let him do so (with his own money, if it's reasonable). When your daughter spills ketchup all over your newspaper and wants to wipe it off so you can read it, let her (even though you may need to wait fifteen minutes for her to finish until you can read the paper). The mess and wait are well worth it. When your children wake you up when you're sick or have a headache, don't shut down their professed wish to now be quiet for the rest of day by telling them that it's too late, that you've already lost your opportunity for a good night's sleep. Let them spend the day trying to be quiet enough so that you can make up for the sleep they denied you earlier that morning.

And when they say something mean to you in anger, let them take it back and say they didn't mean it. And let them treat you nicely for the rest of the morning, if that is their way of making amends.

Many children react to their misbehavior and misdeeds by experiencing an avalanche of shame, an emotion that can lead them to dig a deeper hole for themselves. Help teach your children how to get out of such quicksand when they get into trouble or hurt another person's feelings. Demonstrate how you do it.

There is no one right way to say sorry or make amends that we need to teach our children. The right way is the way that they feel it inside, the remorse and regret they know, and the desire to make it right, whatever that means, in their judgment. The sincere sorry and amends are what parents want to nurture and promote in their children as they grow from small to large, and as their likely errors grow that way as well. To meet their genuinely apologetic gifts with our respect and gratitude is the most powerful sign of approval and appreciation, and doing so fosters children's growing confidence in their ability to take life on, missteps and all. The following sections provide some guidelines for helping your child feel and show remorse.

There is no one right way to say sorry or make amends.

Give empathy. Try to understand what your child is experiencing. For example, many children who have trouble showing remorse are often vulnerable to feeling great amounts of shame whenever they do something that they perceive as bad. Their sense of badness and shame so overwhelms them that they're unable to go through the steps of feeling bad and making amends. Assume that they feel bad rather than accusing them of being inconsiderate or yelling, "What's the matter with you? You just hurt your sister and you don't even care!" Ouch, that is a load for a child to hear and likely will not help him to feel more for his sister or himself.

Help your child put his feelings into words. Some children who struggle with remorse are, in the current vernacular, less emotionally intelligent. So when they do things that hurt others, they are lost and don't know what to do. "Are you worried that I'll be mad at you?" you can ask. Or "Are you confused what to do now?" or "Would you like help figuring out how to show your sister that you feel bad for hurting her?"

Help your child to develop a wider repertoire. Model ways that your child can handle hurts that she inflicts on others. Gently use real-life opportunities to help educate her on how people deal with errors and mistakes.

Help your child to not be a perfectionist. Perfectionist children are prone to reacting to even the slightest misstep with an avalanche of self-hatred and discouragement that can spill out in aggressive and provocative words or behaviors. Let him know both in words and by your own example that you know life is full of tumbles but that they can often be overcome and repaired. Note your child's attempts at amends, even if they are crude, awkward, full of blame, and so on. He feels bad and in his own limited way is trying to do something about what he said or did.

Lead by example. Some parents, by their own admission, are not so good at saying sorry and making amends. Their children know this, too. The parent's example can be a powerful teacher in several ways. Acknowledge when you hurt your child's feelings, and own up to it. Let your child see and hear you own and take responsibility for the hurts you inflict on other family members. Do you model a grown-up who takes responsibility for his actions and who can express true regret and make genuine amends? Can you move on once you have done so, or are you forever apologizing and indulging as a way to assuage your guilt? (Some perfectionist parents cannot tolerate being anything less than ideal, a surefire way to make sure they will always feel inadequate and overcompensate to their child's detriment.) And last, do you ever demonstrate that relationships can be repaired and that doing so can make them even stronger?

Take your sorries, regrets, and guilt over your overindulgent parenting and use them as fuel to turbo-power your efforts and conviction to unspoil.

Parenthood is the passing of a baton, followed by a lifelong disagreement as to who dropped it.

—ROBERT BRAULT

24. Collaborate

WHEN IT COMES TO PARENTING, some couples really get their groove going. They share the same values and expectations. Both parents had good parents of their own who taught them good ways to raise children. With the seamless synchrony of Viennese waltzers, they parent together, alternatively, and side by side as if they'd choreographed and rehearsed every step. Each parent feels supported and never undermined by the other parent. Each seems to watch the other's parenting back with a sixth sense.

But you and I and most everyone else I know are

not that blessed and golden parenting couple. Nor were Mr. and Mrs. W. Whenever we met it was the same. Mrs. W. shamefully avowed the spoiling she'd done. "I bought them gum anyway." "I can't believe it myself. I still took them to the fair." "Even after all they'd done, I made them brownies." After each confession, Mr. W. rolled his eyes, shook his head, and rubbed his brow in disapproval.

Mr. W. would ever say something like, "She just doesn't get it." Then, with Mrs. W leading the way, we'd problem solve, helping her to not spoil the children, who were considerably out of control. But some sessions later, a bigger and different truth came out.

"How could you let the three of them do that? I don't understand." Mrs. W. spoke with visible upset. Mr. W. looked at the floor. "I let myself get a job for one Saturday afternoon and now I have to worry that I can't leave the house?" Through tears, Mrs. W. described coming home to find a mess beyond belief. Nacho cheese and ketchup on the couch, spilled soda, empty soda cans on the floor, model glue on the table, paint on the rug. "I'd just cleaned the whole house on Friday!"

"They're boys," Mr. W. defended himself sheepishly.

But Mrs. W. knew all about boys. She mothered three of them, and she'd grown up with brothers. She was a bona fide expert on boys' curiosity, energy, and adventurousness. But she wasn't dealing with "boys will be boys." This was Huckleberry Finn meets the seed of Chucky, times three.

"You're worse than the boys!" she accused.

"You have no idea what it's like being with them for a whole day," Mr. W. blurted.

It took several minutes of silence and tension before the two of them broke into laughter.

"I don't know how she does it," Mr. W. looked at the ceiling. "It's too much for me."

Forget what *Redbook* says about candles and satin sheets. There's absolutely nothing more seductive in a relationship than blaming the other person. Remember, it usually takes two to spoil, just as it usually takes two to unspoil. Don't be fooled into thinking that you

There's absolutely nothing more seductive in a relationship than blaming the other person.

are the good parent, the unspoiler and your partner is the bad parent, the spoiler. It's nearly always more complicated that way. In general, the parent who does the lion's share of caretaking and nurturing is prone to indulge more, especially when worn out. Beware of critiquing the other until you've tried doing what she or he does for a few weeks, day in and day out.

Remember that spoiling can be a natural extension of loving and good parenting. True, you'd prefer your well-loved child to be less spoiled (and that's why you're reading this book). However, you would never want your child raised in an unspoiling home that was void of love, warmth, giving, and pleasure.

If upon scrutiny and honest self-appraisal you assess that you are truly the healthily unspoiling parent, then you want to do all you can to support and win your other over to your unspoiling way of life. (I say "healthily" to distinguish you from parents whose stern, joyless, and withholding brand of unspoiling is more worrisome than good.) We know for certain that blame and criticism probably aren't the way to succeed in your mission. And—do I have to say it?—the laws of spoiling and unspoiling apply equally to all parents, whatever their race, religion, sexual orientation, or marital status.

> To solve disagreements, strive to be positive, rely on "I" statements, take your partner's perspective, look in the mirror, note effort in the right direction, and sometimes mind your own business.

Set frequent times to discuss your parenting and your children in private. Be careful not to use the children as a vehicle for waging greater strife with your spouse. Some parents who grew up in homes where they were traumatized or deprived of their own confirmation desperately need an ally no matter what the conflict in their life. They may, in fact, want to discuss things only when the children are around. Using children as allies, however, can override their needs and put them in psychological peril.

When your spouse indulges in a way that you think is unhealthy, try not to bring it up right then. Arguing in front of your child is not likely to bring the change you'd like and will stress and confuse your child. This is a matter for the grown-ups to settle.

If you are divorced or separated, work hard to keep your child's well-being and unspoiling above the fray and hurt. Although that may require close to saintliness, it is a most loving gift to your child.

Yes, it can be frustrating. But your patience is well founded and to be commended. Few moments of parenting are urgent. One more indulgence is not going to harm your child. Indulgence is a long-term process full of thousands of moments. Your child does not need to be rescued. Later on, when you are settled, set up the conditions for a discussion with your spouse. Share your frustration. "I know you love our child as much as I do, and that you are every bit as good a parent. And I am not willing to argue or criticize you in front of Jamie. But I just don't know how to get my feelings across so you can hear them." You know how best to speak for yourself.

Children can become an easy and permanent distraction for unhappy marriages. It is a burden for children and only prolongs the strife. Taking care of your marriage and your partner is an act of love for your children. If it is beyond your own repair, see a professional or read one of the many good self-help books on relationships by such clinicians as John Gottman (*The Seven Principles for Making Marriage Work*).

> *Taking care of your marriage and your partner is an act of love for your children.*

*Gratitude is when a memory is stored
in the heart and not in the mind.*

—Lionel Hampton

25. Give (and Take) Thanks

"Why you—you ungrateful little…" Why do those words come out so glibly and feel so satisfying, even when we type them on a keyboard? We all feel it, I think. Parents love their children so much and give so much that there is almost nothing their children can do to show their gratitude. But that is in the world of feelings.

There's no reason that children should express that kind of thanks. Nor do they owe us anything. We had children. It is their growing up well that is our reward, just as it will be for them with their children.

Nonetheless, I pose the question, What can parents do when their children seem to feel and show no appreciation for anything in their lives? The question raises yet another, deeper question: what, beyond reasons of temperament and constitution, can cause a child not to feel gratitude?

Children who get and get no matter what tend to appreciate less. They tend to take everything for granted. They think, "You may have bought me the world yesterday, but what have you done for me today?" And you respond, "I don't know. Let me see if Venus is for sale."

Children who get and get no matter what tend to appreciate less.

I am an adult who appreciates much. My wife is the same. Our families and childhoods were as different as can be. The added fact that she grew up in wealthy Long Island and I grew up in a working-class city outside of Boston doesn't seem to matter. Together we've asked ourselves, Why do we tend to feel fortunate and thankful for what we get? The only answer we've come up with is that neither of us got a whole lot. There's nothing like not getting to make a person appreciate what they do get.

It makes sense. Skip breakfast and lunch, and your dinner is bound to taste great. Save up for a year to buy a baseball glove, and you will not forget to bring it home from the field. But if you get a truckload of presents for Christmas, by New Year's Day, you won't remember what you got. You might even have started a new list.

> Children who routinely show no sincere appreciation are telling you and others to give them less. Heed the message.

I know that we can't go back to how it used to be, and I'm not sure that doing so would be a good thing even if we could. I do know that we—our kids and ourselves—are victims of a consumer society that is sinister and out of control. Resisting all that, defying corporate America, and not keeping up with the Joneses is a stiff challenge.

How can you teach children to know the value of a dollar? Refuse to buy them sneakers that cost six times the price of your work shoes. Refuse to give them absolute free rein on an expensive menu, especially when they never eat what they order. Refuse to give them allowances that resemble salaries. Insist that they live within the budget of that allowance. Resist buying them so much, and start noticing how many things—toys, clothes, downloadable songs, and snacks—you buy them in a week. (There's a good bet it's at least ten times what you were given at the same age.)

It's also reasonable for parents to work to teach their child the common decorum of showing thanks. Cordial etiquette helps children make their way through the world. Should your child accept something with rudeness or clear disrespect, take it back. No apology or explanation needed, as in this common situation. A parent gives a child his allowance and he grabs it with a disgusted face, some choice remarks, and an attitude that says, "I got my allowance and all my parents gave me was this lousy five dollars." What does the parent usually do? Walk away feeling resentful, foolish, disrespected, and wondering what good the allowance is doing. Instead, the parent might calmly take the allowance back, and say something like, "It's too bad you think so little of your allowance." Put the money back in the wallet with the hope that it works out better next week. Who said allowances are a given, and who said they can't be used to help teach children? The same goes when children receive gifts from friends or relatives.

Model the gratitude you want your children to show.

With all that we can do, are we wrong for still wanting just a little TLC and a few nods for all we do as parents? Surely not. Meanwhile, learn to take heart from the little things. Note the baby steps that your once disorderly son has taken on the road to civilized neatness. Take pride in the way that your daughter helped the neighbors in their time of need (even if it is kindness that is yet to come your way). Smile at the way your children put aside the noisy fracas long enough to set the table without your having had to ask. Celebrate them to yourself and take credit for the change. Way to go, unspoiler!

Yes, there will be occasional moments of true epiphany, rites of passage at which your children's good and unspoiled growth will astound you. And there may even be signs of gratitude along the way.

For most parents, however, the true thank-yous will come much later when the children are grown up and maybe have their own families. You'll look at the good and decent people they have become and know as sure as anything that what you did was appreciated and worth it.

For most parents, the true thank-yous come much later.

*The thing that impresses me the most about
America is the way parents obey their children.*

—KING EDWARD VIII

26. Claim Your Rights

WHEN WE THINK of unspoiling children, we tend to
think in terms of the child. In fact, when today's parents think of anything, it is often in terms of their children. What about the parents? I ask not just for your
own sake but also for your child's sake. Not expecting
and demanding your parental rights can boomerang,
depriving you and your child.

Not insisting on a position of authority and respect
can teach your child how not to get along with authority. In particular, a mother's not demanding respect or
tolerating abusive mistreatment from a son can put him

at risk for growing into a teen, and eventually a man, who mistreats women, especially women he is close to. Fathers or partners who either model or, through their lack of challenge, implicitly endorse such behavior also contribute to this, just as do mothers who teach their children to disrespect fathers.

> What does devoting all of your time and attention to your children, to the exclusion of your partner, teach them about relationships and being a grown-up?

You deserve appreciation for what you do. Do not allow yourself to be a thankless doormat to be walked over. I know that you can't force gratitude from a child. You can, however, refuse to drive your child to meet friends at the movies when just an hour ago she verbally ripped you apart. I understand the tumult that teens go through, and I'm not suggesting a policy of tough love or rejection. Parents will likely lose that battle. But I am suggesting something subtler. Eleanor

Roosevelt said, "No one can make you feel inferior without your consent." There's a corollary in there for parents, too. If adults don't stick up for themselves, who will, and what does that convey to children about their own self-worth?

Parents deserve private times and places that exclude their child. I hear of children who have free rein of their parents' rooms and stuff any minute of any day. I see children who view their mother's pocketbooks as their own. There are parents who never know a moment in bed together without their child. Allowing children open access to every aspect of parents' lives can make for children who simply cannot bear the idea of their parents having experiences, relationships, and more that exclude them. The more access and control they're given, the more they need, and insatiably so. These children's needs grow out of anxiety and desperate intolerance, as if sharing their parents or being shut out in any way would mean that they were not loved or that someone else were loved instead or more.

Parents deserve to dote on not just children but also on their spouse, partner, and self. Seeing one's parent in a good and loving relationship is generally a healthy and good thing for children. The complete child-centered focus that can dominate some homes can put stress and strain on a marriage. Mothers and fathers need some love and attention, too.

You, as a parent, deserve to trust your own judgment concerning parenting matters. Domestic democracy, in which children have an equal vote, has its place. But that place is not everywhere or all the time. If your child ran the home, just imagine what you'd be eating for supper and doing instead of going to school. (Oops, I didn't mean to embarrass you—I had no idea you're having hot-fudge sundaes for dinner tonight.)

You deserve to have interests beyond your child. Sadly, there are homes in which parents' work, social lives, travel, fitness regimens, and so on leave little time and energy for children. That is a whole other problem.

You deserve to have interests beyond your child.

Here I am referring to parents who forgo everything that matters to them because they devote every free moment and free molecule to the children's well-being and enrichment.

You deserve to consider what you want while making family and personal decisions. Why should the children always pick the restaurant

You deserve understanding and acceptance, too.

or the movie or the book to read? *Always* is the key here. Can you imagine any unwanted lessons that a child might take away from watching parents never state or follow their genuine needs or wishes?

Hardly last and supremely paramount, you deserve forgiveness, your own and the children's, for your inevitable moments of moodiness and impatience, for your mistakes and missteps, and for all that is part of the human condition that makes children and their behaviors forgivable. You deserve understanding and acceptance, too, for your imperfection as a parent. A parent's self-acceptance is a gift to children and can help them grow into more self-accepting adults and parents.

Our society is obsessed with leadership. Learning to be able to follow a good leader is a skill at least equal to being a leader. Teach it to your children.

*It kills you to see them grow up. But I guess it
would kill you quicker if they didn't.*

—Barbara Kingsolver

27. Take a Bow

WELL, YOU'VE DONE IT. By now your child should be looking a lot more like the child you were thinking of parenting. And maybe when you look in the mirror, you look a little more like that parent you've wanted to be.

By now you've probably caught on to my little secret. There really is no such thing as unspoiling. In fact, there's really no such word. But don't be mad at me. My ploy meant no harm and was full of the best intentions.

If I'd told you that simple truth on the first page, I fear you wouldn't have given me and my method a fair shake. I fear you would not have believed that you could really unspoil your child.

Unspoiling is nothing more than the absence of spoiling. You didn't have to go back and undo months or years of unspoiling. All you had to do was to stop your unspoiling from that day on. Not that that wasn't a job indeed.

> *Unspoiling is nothing more than the absence of spoiling.*

Children are by nature hopeful, and they are programmed to grow. They sometimes sound as if they give up on their parents and themselves, but they seldom do. They are always searching for the parenting they crave and need, parenting that sets limits and expectations and refuses to spoil them.

You have been working hard to change, and no one recognizes that more than your child. Keep at it. Allow both yourself and your child to change, to do better, to be better. And let the past mistakes go. Consider yourself a spoiler no more.

> Allow yourself to take pride in your unspoiling effort.

Of course, there was much about parenting (and spoiling) that I never covered in this book. That was the price of my wanting my message to come through loud and clear, short and sweet. What matters is that you know you can do it. If you can unspoil your child, you can do just about anything as a parent. It's true.

As life goes on, there'll be many things you'll come to regret. I can promise you, however—and, yes, I do mean promise—that unspoiling your child will

If you can unspoil your child, you can do just about anything as a parent.

not be one of them. As Rudolf Dreikurs put it, "We cannot protect our children from life. Therefore, it is essential that we prepare them for it." That's what you are now well on the road to doing, and no parent can do more.

Don't hesitate to apply your newfound strength, conviction, and creativity to other aspects of your parenting and life.

An Afterword of Caution

THIS BOOK CAN HELP most any home and family. But it can't do everything. Problems that involve abuse, drugs, or alcohol require the special help of counselors, therapy, self-help groups, and so forth. Even should this book improve your relationship with your child, be aware that unremitting distress or troubling behaviors, yours or your child's, may need the help of professionals. Likewise, although the approaches herein can sometimes greatly benefit some children who have greater troubles—and go by assorted names such as *impulsive, distractible, disorganized, bipolar, difficult,* and *oppositional*—they are not substitutes for therapy or other treatments.

Also by Richard Bromfield

*Doing Therapy with Children and Adolescents
with Asperger Syndrome* (Wiley)

Doing Child and Adolescent Psychotherapy (Wiley)

*Playing for Real: Exploring Child Therapy and
the Inner Worlds of Children* (Basil)

Teens in Therapy: Making It Their Own
(W. W. Norton)

*Handle with Care: Understanding Children and
Teachers* (Teachers College Press)

About the Author

RICHARD BROMFIELD, PhD, is a graduate of Bowdoin College and the University of North Carolina at Chapel Hill. A faculty member of Harvard Medical School, he writes about children,

Photo by Susan G. Cohen

psychotherapy, and family life in both professional and popular periodicals. He is in private practice in Boston, Massachusetts.